MCSE CoursePrep ExamGuide/StudyGuide Exam #70-215

Installing, Configuring, and Administering Microsoft Windows 2000 Server

COURSE TECHNOLOGY
THOMSON LEARNING™

Australia • Canada • Mexico • Singapore • Spain • United Kingdom • United States

COURSE TECHNOLOGY
THOMSON LEARNING

MCSE CoursePrep ExamGuide and ***MCSE CoursePrep StudyGuide*** are published by Course Technology.

Managing Editor
Stephen Solomon

Senior Vice President, Publisher
Kristen Duerr

Production Editor
Anne Valsangiacomo

Developmental Editor/Product Manager
Dave George

Associate Product Manager
Elizabeth Wessen

Editorial Assistant
Janet Aras

Marketing Manager
Toby Shelton

Text Designer
GEX Publishing Services

Cover Designer
Betsy Young

Printed in Canada

1 2 3 4 5 WC 02 01 00 99

For more information, contact Course Technology, 25 Thomson Place, Boston, Massachusetts, 02210.

Or find us on the World Wide Web at: www.course.com

ISBN 0-619-01515-2
ISBN 0-619-03497-1

TABLE OF CONTENTS

PREFACE

The *MCSE CoursePrep ExamGuide* and *MCSE CoursePrep StudyGuide* are the very best tools to use to prepare for exam day. These products are intended to be utilized with the core "Guide to" book, *MCSE Guide to Microsoft Windows 2000 Server* (ISBN 0-619-01517-9), written by Michael Palmer, and published by Course Technology. CoursePrep ExamGuide and CoursePrep StudyGuide provide you ample opportunity to practice, drill and rehearse for the exam!

COURSEPREP EXAMGUIDE

The *MCSE CoursePrep ExamGuide for Exam #70-215*, ISBN 0-619-03497-1, provides the essential information you need to master each exam objective. The ExamGuide devotes an entire two-page spread to each certification objective for the exam, helping you understand the objective, and giving you the bottom line information—what you really need to know. Memorize these facts and bulleted points before heading into the exam. In addition, there are several practice test questions for each objective on the right-hand page. That's hundreds of questions to help you practice for the exam! CoursePrep ExamGuide provides the exam fundamentals and gets you up to speed quickly. If you are seeking even more opportunity to practice and prepare, we recommend that you consider our total solution, CoursePrep StudyGuide, which is described below.

COURSEPREP STUDYGUIDE

For those really serious about certification, we offer an even more robust solution—the *MCSE CoursePrep StudyGuide for Exam #70-215*, ISBN 0-619-01515-2. This offering includes all of the same quality material you get with the CoursePrep ExamGuide, including the unique two-page spread, the bulleted memorization points, and the practice questions. In addition, you receive a password valid for 6 months of practice on CoursePrep, a dynamic test preparation tool. The password is found in an envelope in the back cover of the CoursePrep StudyGuide. CoursePrep is a Web-based pool of hundreds of sample test questions. CoursePrep exam simulation software mimics the exact exam environment. The CoursePrep software is flexible, and allows you to practice in several ways as you master the material. Choose from Certification Mode to experience actual exam-day conditions or Study Mode to request answers and explanations to practice questions. Custom Mode lets you set the options for the practice test, including number of questions, content coverage, and ability to request answers and explanation. Follow the instructions on the inside back cover to access the exam simulation software. To see a demo of this dynamic test preparation tool, go to www.courseprep.com.

Features

The *MCSE Course*

Prep ExamGuide and *MCSE CoursePrep StudyGuide* include the following features:

Detailed coverage of the certification objectives in a unique two-page spread. Study strategically by really focusing in on the MCSE certification objectives. To enable you to do this, a two-page spread is devoted to each certification objective. The left-hand page provides the critical facts you need, while the right-hand page features practice questions relating to that objective. You'll find the certification objective(s) and sub-objectives(s) clearly listed in the upper left-hand corner of each spread.

An overview of the objective is provided in the ***Understanding the Objective*** section. Next, ***What you Really Need to Know*** lists bulleted, succinct core facts, skills, and concepts about the objective. Memorizing these facts will be important for your success when taking the exam. ***Objectives on the Job*** places the objective in an industry perspective, and tells you how you can expect to incorporate the objective on the job. This section also provides troubleshooting information.

Practice Test Questions on each right-hand page help you prepare for the exam by testing your skills, identifying your strengths and weaknesses, and demonstrating the subject matter you will face on the exams and how it will be tested. These questions are written in a similar fashion to real MCSE exam questions. The questions test your knowledge of the objectives described on the left-hand page and also the information in the *MCSE Guide to Microsoft Windows 2000 Professional.* Answers to the practice test questions are found at the back of this Guide.

Acronym Glossary: The world of networking, perhaps more than any other computer-related discipline, uses a language all its own, which is comprised largely of acronyms. You will find a complete list of all acronyms used in this Guide, along with their meanings, at the back of the book.

For more information: If you require more information about networking concepts in general, or MCSE exam objectives in particular, please see *MCSE Guide to Microsoft Windows 2000 Server*, by Michael Palmer (Course Technology, 2001)

Section 1

Installing Windows 2000 Server

OBJECTIVES

1.1 Perform an attended installation of Windows 2000 Server

SETUP • REQUIREMENTS • STAGES

UNDERSTANDING THE OBJECTIVE

Attended installations of Windows 2000 are relatively painless, provided that you adhere to the numerous guidelines for installation. You can perform upgrades from earlier Windows NT operating systems or clean installations depending on your needs. Your choice, however, determines the actual installation steps.

WHAT YOU REALLY NEED TO KNOW

- All hardware must appear on the HCL. A somewhat easier alternative is to run WINNT32 /CHECKUPGRADEONLY (comparable to the CHKUPGRD utility), which provides you with a report of the machine's hardware and software compatibility.
- Windows 2000 requires the following at a minimum: a Pentium 133 processor (up to four supported), 128 MB of RAM, and sufficient hard disk space (typically 1 GB or more). Microsoft recommends the following: Pentium II or higher, 256 MB RAM, and 2 GB hard disk space.
- The Setup program can be run by booting from the CD-ROM or while running another operating system, from a network share, or from the Setup boot floppies.
- You can add custom mass storage controller drivers and a **HAL** during setup by pressing the F6 and F5 keys, respectively.
- To install Windows 2000 over a network, create a share point that contains the \I386 directory from the Windows 2000 CD-ROM. From the target computer, connect to the share and run WINNT for MS-DOS and Windows 3.x clients or WINNT32 for Windows 9x and NT clients, or use a network client boot disk where no operating system exists.
- Windows 2000 Server is installed as a member server by default (to reduce administrative overhead). To promote it to a domain controller, run DCPROMO.

OBJECTIVES ON THE JOB

Installation of Windows 2000 Server should proceed without much complication. In addition, Windows 2000 offers full support for Plug and Play, to the same extent as Windows 9x. This feature is a major improvement, as it considerably reduces installation time and administrative effort while performing Windows 2000 installations. Windows 2000 has a driver database containing some 12,000 files, so you should find that your hardware is supported. If this is not the case, you should be able to install the correct driver (supplied by the hardware vendor) during or after setup.

PRACTICE TEST QUESTIONS

1. **You have a stand-alone machine with a clean hard disk on which you wish to install Windows 2000 Server. The system BIOS does not support booting from the CD-ROM drive. How could you proceed?**
   a. Start the installation from a network installation share.
   b. Start the installation from the resident operating system.
   c. Start the installation from the four boot floppy disks.
   d. Run WINNT32 from the CD-ROM.
2. **What are the minimum hardware requirements for installing Windows 2000 Server? (Choose all that apply.)**
   a. A Pentium 133 processor
   b. A Pentium 90 processor
   c. 64 MB of RAM
   d. 128 MB of RAM
3. **You have a third-party mass storage controller in your new system on which you intend to install Windows 2000 Server. You need to provide the installation with a custom driver for this device during setup. What steps should you take?**
   a. During text-based setup, specify the custom driver by pressing "S" at the appropriate screen.
   b. When you see the message, "Setup is inspecting your computer's hardware configuration," press F6.
   c. During GUI-based setup, install the custom driver.
   d. Boot the machine from the third-party vender-supplied boot disk, and install the supplied driver.
4. **You wish to install a fresh copy of Windows 2000 Server on an old, unused legacy system for testing purposes. You are unsure whether Windows 2000 Server will support the components on the system. How can you verify their functionality? (Choose all that apply.)**
   a. Run WINNT /CHECKUPGRADEONLY.
   b. Ensure that all the components appear on the HCL.
   c. Run WINNT32 /CHECKUPGRADEONLY.
   d. Run CHKUPGRD.
5. **Windows 2000 Server is installed as a domain controller by default.**
   a. True
   b. False
6. **Windows 2000 member servers can be promoted to domain controllers by using the DCPROMO utility.**
   a. True
   b. False

OBJECTIVES

1.2 Perform an unattended installation of Windows 2000 Server

PARAMETERS • ANSWER FILE • DEPLOYMENT

UNDERSTANDING THE OBJECTIVE

Natively, Windows 2000 supports numerous methods to automate the deployment of both the Professional and Server versions of the opertaing system. Depending on which method you choose, (Sysprep, Syspart, **SMS**, bootable CD, or Unattended), the setup process will be influenced by the criteria you define. This objective discusses the latter option and explains how to perform such an installation.

WHAT YOU REALLY NEED TO KNOW

- Unattended installation requires three key elements: a correctly configured distribution folder, an answer (.txt) file, and the requisite Windows 2000 setup commands.
- The distribution folder must be a network share with the \I386 folder on the Windows 2000 CD copied to a directory at the root of the share, typically called the \I386 directory, (although other names work equally well). Directly under the \I38 folder, you should create the \OEM subfolder, which must maintain this name.
- The answer file is a text file that can have any name, but is ordinarily called UNATTEND.TXT. It contains answers to the questions that Setup asks the user in an attended installation, thus automating the process. The UNATTEND.DOC file on the Windows 2000 CD gives full configuration details for this file (found in \Support\tools\deploy.cab).
- Use WINNT for a clean installation with MS-DOS or Windows 3.x.
- Use WINNT32 for an upgrade or clean installation with Windows 9x and NT.
- Use WINNT /S[:*sourcepath*] /U[:*answer_file*] for unattended installations. A maximum of eight /S switches are supported to speed up file copying and load balancing for multiple unattended installations.
- To automate the installation of server applications immediately after Setup completes, use the CMDLINE.TXT file (which must reside in the \OEM subfolder of the distribution share) or the [GuiRunOnce] section of the answer file.
- You can use the answer file with the **ADIW** in one of two ways: run the DCPROMO command from the [GuiRunOnce] section of the answer file, or create a special answer file for ADIW and run DCPROMO /ANSWER:*answer_file_name*.

OBJECTIVES ON THE JOB

Unattended Windows 2000 setup is a viable option for automating installations. Answer files can be used to set configuration options such as passwords and to extend NTFS hard disk partitions among many other configuration settings.

PRACTICE TEST QUESTIONS

1. **You wish to perform five new Windows 2000 Server unattended installations on your network. The new machines have blank hard disks, and you intend to connect to the distribution share that contains the setup files using an MS-DOS network boot disk from each computer. What command should you run to initiate the setup process?**
   a. WINNT with the /S and /UNATTEND switches
   b. WINNT with the /S and /U switches
   c. WINNT32 with the /S and /U switches
   d. WINNT32 with the /S and /UNATTEND switches
2. **Which of the following is an answer file that could be used in an unattended setup?**
   a. UNATTEND.BAT
   b. UNATTEND.UDF
   c. UNATTEND.INF
   d. ATTEND.TXT
3. **You are planning an unattended setup for 20 Windows 2000 Servers on your network. The installation machines have the latest Ethernet network adapters installed. How can you ensure that the installation uses the vendor-supplied network card drivers? (Choose all that apply.)**
   a. Ensure that the [Unattend] section of the answer file contains the entry OEMPreinstall=YES.
   b. Ensure that the [Unattend] section of the answer file contains the entry OEMBrivers=YES.
   c. Include the driver in the \$OEM$\$1\<pnpdrivers>directory.
   d. Include the driver in the \OEM\<pnpdrivers>directory.
4. **What is the required directory structure of the distribution share for the files used in an unattended setup?**
   a. <share root>\<I386 files>\OEM
   b. I386\OEM
   c. OEM\I386
   d. <share root>\OEM
5. **You want to automate the installation of server applications after your unattended installation of Windows 2000 Server is complete. How can you achieve this goal? (Choose all that apply.)**
   a. Place the CMDLINES.TXT file in the \$autoinstall$ subfolder of the distribution share.
   b. Specify the applications you want to install in the [GuiRunOnce] section of the answer file.
   c. Specify the applications you want to install in the [AutoInstall] section of the answer file.
   d. Place the CMDLINES.TXT file in the \OEM subfolder of the distribution share.

OBJECTIVES

1.3 Create unattended answer files by using Setup Manager to automate the installation of Windows 2000 Server

SETUP MANAGER WIZARD • ANSWER FILES • DEPLOYMENT

UNDERSTANDING THE OBJECTIVE

Although unattended installations provide an effective way to deploy Windows 2000, it can be an extremely laborious process to create the prerequisite answer files necessary to effect this procedure. Microsoft offers a utility that greatly simplifies this process and brings additional functionality to the process as a whole, known as the **SMW**.

WHAT YOU REALLY NEED TO KNOW

- The SMW assists Administrators in three ways: it can create answer files used in the automated deployment of Windows 2000, extract configuration information from a preconfigured machine into an answer file, and create distribution folders with the correct directory structure for unattended installations (a time-saving exercise).
- SMW can create new answer files and modify existing ones. It can also duplicate the configuration of the machine on which it is installed.
- Five unattended modes can be specified in SMW: Provide defaults—user can amend default answers during installation; Fully automated—no user intervention; Hide pages—user sees only dialogs that require input: Read only—dialogs are displayed, but user intervention is forbidden; GUI attended—only the text-based mode of setup is automated, and the GUI requires user input.
- SMW creates three files: UNATTEND.BAT, UNATTEND.TXT, and UNATTEND.UDF.
- SMW creates a batch file to demonstrate how the answer file it also produces works. You may need to edit this batch file if the answer file or distribution share has been relocated, for example.
- If you specify multiple computer names in SMW, a .udf file is created that contains the computer name data. This file must be included in the Windows 2000 setup parameters—for example, WINNT32 /S /UNATTEND /UDF or WINNT /S /U /UDF.

OBJECTIVES ON THE JOB

Using SMW to create answer files and distribution folders greatly enhances and simplifies the automated installation of Windows 2000, and it can reduce the tedium involved in manually creating specific answer files. It is essential that you experiment with this wizard to get a good grasp of its capabilities. You can find SMW and its attendant help files either on the Windows 2000 CD in DEPLOY.CAB in the support/tools directory or in the Windows 2000 Server Resource Kit.

PRACTICE TEST QUESTIONS

1. **What are the three basic uses for the Setup Manager Wizard?**
    a. Creating answer files
    b. Generating unique SIDs for target machines that have been cloned
    c. Creating distribution directories
    d. Extracting existing configuration information into an answer file
2. **You do not want users to see the default information that you have entered in the Setup Manager Wizard for a Windows 2000 unattended installation, but you want them to input information in dialogs where you have not specified any information. Which mode should you select in the wizard?**
    a. Read only
    b. Hide pages
    c. Fully automated
    d. GUI attended
3. **You have used the Setup Manager Wizard to create an answer file for your unattended installation of five Windows 2000 Server computers. You realize that you inadvertently omitted one computer, so you now wish to add it to the unattended installation. How could you accomplish this task?**
    a. Manually edit the UNATTEND.TXT file
    b. Manually edit the UNATTEND.UDF file
    c. Manually edit the UNATTEND.BAT file
    d. Manually edit the UNATTEND.SIF file
4. **Which three files does the Setup Manager Wizard create if multiple computer names are specified for an unattended Windows 2000 installation?**
    a. UNATTEND.TXT
    b. UNATTEND.UDF
    c. UNATTEND.BAT
    d. UNATTEND.INF
5. **You use the Setup Manager Wizard to create answer files for unattended installations of Windows 2000 Server. After the wizard completes the process, you move the distribution share to another server located on your network. What needs to be done now?**
    a. Manually edit the UNATTEND.TXT file to point to the new location
    b. Manually edit the UNATTEND.UDF file to point to the new location
    c. Manually edit the UNATTEND.BAT file to point to the new location
    d. Nothing

OBJECTIVES

1.4 Create and configure automated methods for installation of Windows 2000

AUTOMATION • TECHNIQUES • DEPLOYMENT

UNDERSTANDING THE OBJECTIVE

Unattended installations are not the only way to automate installations of Windows 2000; indeed, they represent only the basis or one alternative for an effective automated deployment solution. In fact, you can choose any of four main paths to automate Windows 2000 Server installations.

WHAT YOU REALLY NEED TO KNOW

- If you have multiple computers with dissimilar hardware, you can pass the /SYSPART parameter to WINNT32 to create a master set of files with the required configuration and driver support. These files can then be cloned to dissimilar hardware systems, thereby ensuring the correct setup of the base operating system. Syspart can be used only for clean installations.
- The Sysprep utility is an excellent choice for disk imaging of machines with identical hardware, but not necessarily Plug and Play devices. It is used in conjunction with third-party hardware or software disk imaging solutions to prepare the source computer for cloning and can be used on both upgraded systems and clean installations. Sysprep uses a Mini-Setup Wizard that runs on the first boot of the cloned operating system. It also generates a new machine SID, thereby overcoming a major shortcoming of disk imaging.
- **SMS** presents a total management solution for upgrading from previous versions of Windows to Windows 2000. The main benefit of this option relates to the centralized control given to an Administrator when an actual upgrade takes place, such as after data backups or training.
- The bootable CD distribution is useful where, for example, remote offices have slow links. Provided the target machine's BIOS supports booting from the CD, you can use this method of deployment. Such an installation requires an answer file named WINNT.SIF to be located on a floppy disk and passed to Windows 2000 setup during the blue text-mode phase. This answer file must contain a [Data] section with the required keys.

OBJECTIVES ON THE JOB

You must become familiar with the multitude of automated Windows 2000 Server installation procedures. Quite possibly, the only way to achieve this goal may involve hands-on experience. It is strongly recommended that you run through a few iterations of each setup technique, with one exception. While you should know the purpose of SMS, it is unlikely that the exam will include any questions on this sophisticated product.

PRACTICE TEST QUESTIONS

1. **Which automated methods can you use to produce a clean installation of Windows 2000 Server? (Choose all that apply.)**
   a. WINNT32 /SYSPART
   b. SYSPREP.EXE
   c. Systems Management Server
   d. Bootable CD
2. **Which other parameter must you use with Syspart for a successful installation?**
   a. /t
   b. /td
   c. /tempdrive
   d. No other parameter is required
3. **Active Directory components cannot be duplicated using Sysprep.**
   a. True
   b. False
4. **What are Sysprep's optional parameters? (Choose all that apply.)**
   a. /quiet
   b. /nosidgen
   c. /reboot
   d. /q
5. **What is the purpose of the SYSPREP.INF file?**
   a. It automates all or part of the Mini-Setup Wizard process.
   b. It is the mandatory answer file employed when setting up the source computer for disk imaging using Sysprep.
   c. It is the optional answer file employed when setting up the source computer for disk imaging using Sysprep.
   d. It is a mandatory file that must be present in the same directory as the Sysprep utility.
6. **You are using Sysprep to prepare a Windows 2000 Server for disk imaging. You wish to use a SYSPREP.INF file to change the administrative password in the Mini-Setup Wizard. What condition must prevail for this configuration to function?**
   a. The SYSPREP.INF file must be located in the same directory as SYSPREP.EXE.
   b. The existing administrative password must be blank.
   c. SETUPCL.EXE must be present in the same directory as SYSPREP.INF.
   d. The WINNT.SIF file must be present in the same directory as the Sysprep utility.

OBJECTIVES

1.5 Upgrade a server from Windows NT 4.0

COMPATIBILITY • UPGRADE PATHS • SERVER TYPES

UNDERSTANDING THE OBJECTIVE

To retain the existing network configuration, among other reasons, you can follow the Windows 2000 upgrade path rather than performing a clean installation of Windows 2000. Windows 2000 permits upgrades of all types of Windows NT 4.0 **DCs**, member servers, and standalone servers. Many factors inherent in any particular network influence which of these servers should be migrated first to Windows 2000, but some rules need to be followed to achieve successful migration.

WHAT YOU REALLY NEED TO KNOW

- Only WINNT32 can be used to upgrade Windows NT 4.0 Servers.
- You can upgrade Windows NT 4.0 Server and NT 4.0 Terminal Server to Windows 2000 Server, but NT 4.0 Enterprise Edition can be upgraded only to Windows 2000 Advanced Server.
- Two alternatives for upgrading to Windows 2000 exist: upgrade DCs first or upgrade member servers first.
- If upgrading NT 4.0 DCs initially, the **PDC** must be upgraded first. If a member server currently acts as a remote access server, it is recommended that it be upgraded to Windows 2000 before the last DC is upgraded.
- Once the conversion of all NT 4.0 DCs to Windows 2000 is complete, you have the option of converting from mixed mode (the coexistence of NT 4.0 DCs and Windows 2000 DCs) to native mode (strictly Windows 2000 DCs, but any other clients and servers). This change is a one-time and irreversible conversion.
- The order of server upgrades determines which Windows 2000 features are available. If DCs are upgraded initially, then the features of AD will be present (in addition to others like Group Policy and security authentication). This process requires the organization of **AD** structures at the time of upgrade. If member servers are upgraded first, many features are still available, with the notable exception of AD.

OBJECTIVES ON THE JOB

It is difficult to give specific advice on managed Windows 2000 upgrades, as each network is different. Obviously, common practices should prevail, such as backing up all servers before an upgrade and ensuring that the hard disk has sufficient disk space for the installation. Windows 2000 setup can expand the existing NT 4.0 user accounts database to 10 times its original size when the database is converted to Windows 2000 format. To protect your existing NT 4.0 environment, ensure that a **BDC** has an up-to-date user account database, back it up, and remove it from the network before upgrading the PDC to Windows 2000. Should the upgrade of the PDC fail, you can promote this BDC to a PDC if required.

PRACTICE TEST QUESTIONS

1. **You are upgrading a Windows NT 4.0 member server to Windows 2000 Server. You run through the setup procedure, but no upgrade option is available and Windows 2000 is installed in a separate %systemroot% directory. Why?**
   a. The Windows NT 4.0 %systemroot% directory resides on a FAT partition.
   b. You can upgrade only Windows NT 4.0 domain controllers.
   c. You ran WINNT instead of WINNT32.
   d. You selected the "Multi-boot" option in text-based setup.

2. **Which platforms can you upgrade to Windows 2000 Server? (Choose all that apply.)**
   a. Windows NT 4.0 Server
   b. Windows NT 4.0 Terminal Server
   c. Windows NT 4.0 Enterprise Edition
   d. Windows BackOffice Small Business Server

3. **You are trying to upgrade a Windows NT 4.0 domain controller to Windows 2000 Server. You boot from the CD, but Setup does not present an upgrade option. Why?**
   a. You selected the "Multi-boot" option in the text-based setup.
   b. You should use the boot floppies when performing an upgrade installation.
   c. You must run WINNT32 from within the operating system that you wish to upgrade.
   d. The Windows NT 4.0 domain controller is corrupted, so the upgrade installation option is unavailable.

4. **How should you upgrade Windows NT 4.0 domain controllers to Windows 2000 Server?**
   a. No particular order is preferred; domain controller upgrades can occur in an arbitrary manner.
   b. Upgrade the BDCs first, then the remaining primary domain controller. If a remote access member server exists, upgrade it before upgrading the Windows NT 4.0 primary domain controller.
   c. Upgrade the primary domain controller first, then the remaining domain controllers. If a remote access member server exists, upgrade it before upgrading the last Windows NT 4.0 backup domain controller.
   d. If a remote access member server exists, upgrade it before undertaking domain controller migration to Windows 2000.

5. **You have a heterogeneous network of Windows NT 4.0 and Windows 2000 domain controllers. You upgrade all of the Windows NT 4.0 domain controllers to Windows 2000 domain controllers. What should you do to ensure that all domain controllers can take advantage of the universal and nested group features of Windows 2000?**
   a. Convert to mixed mode
   b. Convert to native mode
   c. Revert from native mode to mixed mode
   d. Convert to mixed/native mode

OBJECTIVES

1.6 Deploy service packs

SERVICE PACKS • SYSTEMS MANAGEMENT SERVER • DISTRIBUTION • SLIPSTREAMING

UNDERSTANDING THE OBJECTIVE

The deployment of service packs or critical updates is an important aspect of maintaining the integrity of a Windows 2000 network. Several paths are available to the Administrator for instituting and implementing an efficient deployment solution for service packs. Understanding the key elements of each path is crucial in deciding the most suitable distribution method.

WHAT YOU REALLY NEED TO KNOW

- Windows 2000 service packs are available from the Microsoft Web site, from the FTP site, via CD-ROM, or through the Windows Update utility.
- Service packs can be installed over the Internet (Windows Update), from a network share, or directly from a CD-ROM. To initiate network and CD installations, run UPDATE.EXE, which is found in the \I386\update folder.
- Windows 2000 enables service packs to be slipstreamed into existing Windows 2000 installation shares. Slipstreaming allows service pack code to be incorporated into Windows 2000 installations without requiring subsequent installation of the service pack. Currently, this deployment method is supported only on clean installations.
- SMS advertises the availability of service packs to each of its clients and installs these service packs, automatically rebooting the client system to make it ready for logon.
- Windows Installer is a recent innovation from Microsoft for deploying software. You use Windows Installer Technology to create packages, which have the file extension .msi. To manage Windows Installer packages, use the Group Policy.
- Service packs can be uninstalled in Windows 2000. In such a case, the system reverts to its original state prior to a service pack upgrade.

OBJECTIVES ON THE JOB

Numerous routes to deploying Windows 2000 service packs exist. Running Windows Update comes with a caveat: you must have administrative privileges to update any machines. Without such privileges, installation of system files is not feasible. Use service pack slipstreaming to include service pack code in multiple, clean Windows 2000 installations. Deploying service packs to an existing Windows 2000 user base is a different matter. If the network is equipped with SMS, you can wrap the service pack in a SMS package and advertise it to your users. Alternatively, you can create a network share or use Windows Installer Technology. For stand-alone machines, a CD installation is relatively simple and usually complication-free.

PRACTICE TEST QUESTIONS

1. **You wish to update your Windows 2000 Server to the latest service pack. You log on to the server and run Windows Update, but Windows Update does not function. What could cause this problem? (Choose all that apply.)**
   a. You must be logged on as a member of the Administrators group.
   b. You must be logged on as a member of the Server Operators group, at a minimum.
   c. Windows Update needs to install an ActiveX control, and Internet Explorer's security settings are configured to prevent this installation.
   d. You have not enabled the "Allow updates from Microsoft's web site" setting in Internet Explorer.
2. **You are a corporate administrator and want to slipstream a service pack into a Windows 2000 installation network share so as to install the service pack on five Windows 2000 Server computers. What parameters should you pass to UPDATE.EXE?**
   a. /n
   b. /u
   c. /slip:<*directory*>
   d. /slipstream:<*directory*>
3. **You are the Administrator of a Windows 2000 network. You must install the latest service pack on 50 Windows 2000 Servers. What technique can you use to accomplish this task? (Choose all that apply.)**
   a. Use Systems Management Server to advertise a service pack package to the SMS client-enabled servers.
   b. Make the service pack available to the servers from a network share and run UPDATE.EXE on each server.
   c. Attend each server and perform a CD-based service pack installation.
   d. Slipstream the service pack into a network share and run UPDATE.EXE on all servers.
4. **You have a network containing only Windows 2000 Server and Professional machines. You want to distribute the latest Windows 2000 service pack to these machines so that it is installed at next logon. How could you accomplish this task?**
   a. Add the service pack to Active Directory to automate its distribution.
   b. Incorporate the package into Autologon using Windows Installer Technology.
   c. Configure the Group Policy using Windows Installer Technology.
   d. Configure the Local Policy using Windows Installer Technology.
5. **How are Windows 2000 service packs made available? (Choose all that apply.)**
   a. They are downloadable from the Microsoft Web site.
   b. They are downloadable from the Microsoft FTP site.
   c. They are found on CD-ROMs available from Microsoft.
   d. They are available through the Windows Update program.

OBJECTIVES

1.7 Troubleshoot failed installations

SAFE MODE OPTIONS • RECOVERY CONSOLE • REPAIR • EMERGENCY REPAIR DISK

UNDERSTANDING THE OBJECTIVE

Knowing how to recover from a failed Windows 2000 installation is an an essential part of effective systems administration. Windows 2000 expands on the Windows NT 4.0 recovery feature set by providing enhancements and improvements that give the Administrator a comprehensive array of tools for efficient system recovery. You must know how to utilize these tools so as to quickly identify and diagnose problems, not only for the exam, but also for general Windows 2000 systems administration.

WHAT YOU REALLY NEED TO KNOW

- As an Administrator, you can use one of three main options when a Windows 2000 computer does not start: safe mode options, the **RC**, and the **ERD**.
- Safe mode options are available only during Windows 2000 system start-up. Press F8 after the boot menu to access the list of safe mode options, including Last Known Good Configuration.
- The RC is a powerful command-line-based tool that is accessed during system setup or from the boot menu (if installed). To access the RC, rerun Windows 2000 Setup from the CD-ROM or Setup disks, then select the Repair option.
- The ERD is similar to Windows NT 4.0's ERD. It is also performed by rerunning setup and selecting Repair.
- You must have administrative privileges to use the RC. The RC possesses powerful commands that help an Administrator restore or repair a Windows 2000 installation. Enter/? on the command line to obtain a list of commands. Two especially important commands are fixboot and fixbr.
- To create an ERD, use the backup program in Windows 2000. The disk contains only three files: AUTOEXEC.NT, CONFIG.NT, and SETUP.LOG.

OBJECTIVES ON THE JOB

Starting a computer in safe mode is useful when, for example, a new device driver is causing problems or error messages. From safe mode, you can delete the updated driver and restore the old, or another, driver. The RC does not provide unlimited access to folders in a Windows 2000 installation. The %windir% is (virtually) the only directory that you can access. Nevertheless, the commands that can be utilized are very effective, such as fixboot and fixmbr, which can be used to repair boot sectors and partition tables, respectively.

PRACTICE TEST QUESTIONS

1. **You have modified the partition configuration of your Windows 2000 computer. Now the computer doesn't start and you wish to alter the BOOT.INI file to correct the problem. How can you accomplish this task?**
   a. Use the safe mode with Command Prompt start-up option to modify the BOOT.INI file.
   b. Use the Recovery Console to modify the BOOT.INI file.
   c. Use safe mode to select the Last Known Good Configuration option.
   d. Repair the installation with the Emergency Repair Disk.
2. **You have changed the Registry by using the regedit command. When you try to restart your Windows 2000 computer to implement the changes, you are unable to do so. How can you quickly recover the previous configuration settings?**
   a. Use the Emergency Repair Disk to restore a copy of the Registry.
   b. Use the Emergency Repair Disk to edit the Registry.
   c. Enter safe mode options and select Safe Mode.
   d. Enter safe mode options and select Last Known Good Configuration.
3. **Which files are present on an Emergency Repair Disk? (Choose all that apply.)**
   a. AUTOEXEC.NT
   b. CONFIG.NT
   c. SETUP.LOG
   d. SAM.EXE
4. **You want to write a new boot sector to your NTFS system partition, as you are receiving error messages that suggest it has become corrupted. How can you achieve this goal?**
   a. Use the Recovery Console to run the fixbr command.
   b. Use the Recovery Console to run the fixboot command.
   c. Use the Emergency Repair Disk to replace the boot files.
   d. Boot the machine with a bootable DOS disk and run FDISK /MBR.
5. **You wish to restore Active Directory on a Windows 2000 domain controller. You enter safe mode options at start-up. Which option should you select?**
   a. Directory Service Restore Mode
   b. Active Directory Service Restore Mode
   c. AD Restore
   d. Debugging Mode
6. **You want to replace the master boot code of the boot partition. How could you accomplish this task?**
   a. Enter the Recovery Console and execute the fixboot command.
   b. Enter the Recovery Console and execute the fixbr command.
   c. Enter the Recovery Console and execute the FDISK /MBR command.
   d. Enter safe mode with Command Prompt and execute the FDISK /MBR command.

Section 2

Installing, Configuring and Troubleshooting Access to Resources

OBJECTIVES

2.1 Install network services

NETWORK SERVICES • DHCP • DNS • WINS

UNDERSTANDING THE OBJECTIVE

Installing the **DHCP**, **DNS**, and **WINS** services allows you to enhance the efficiency of your network and reduce administrative overhead. In Windows 2000, you can use DHCP to install Windows 2000 Professional on machines through the **RIS** service. DNS is required on a network using Active Directory services. WINS is required if the network includes down-level clients or applications that use NetBIOS names.

WHAT YOU REALLY NEED TO KNOW

- DNS must be installed if you want to use a Windows 2000 domain controller.
- Three DNS zone types exist: Active Directory-integrated, standard primary, and standard secondary.
- The first zone created must be the primary zone.
- Domain names may include a maximum of 63 characters, including periods. Short names allow you to avoid using the underscore character (_).
- The DHCP server must be authorized with the Active Directory services.
- At least one forward lookup zone must be configured to run the DNS service. Reverse lookup zones are required to run some of the troubleshooting tools, such as NSLOOKUP.
- WINS has four node types. Choose the H-node, which indicates that the WINS server should be checked before sending a broadcast.
- Place WINS proxies on subnets that broadcast name requests. A WINS proxy queries the WINS server and returns the results to the requesting client.
- All network services are installed using the Windows Component Wizard.

OBJECTIVES ON THE JOB

DHCP is very useful for medium-size to large organizations. It is also required to take advantage of many of the new features in Windows 2000, such as RIS installations. In addition, DHCP allows you to give clients the address for the WINS server, the DNS server, and the default gateway. A DNS server is necessary for accessing the Internet. WINS is needed to support down-level clients.

PRACTICE TEST QUESTIONS

1. **Which service resolves NetBIOS names to IP addresses?**
   a. DHCP
   b. DNS
   c. Dynamic DNS
   d. WINS
2. **When you run DC promo, what service must exist on your network?**
   a. DDNS
   b. DHCP
   c. DNS
   d. WINS
3. **Which types of records exist for the DNS server after the initial installation? (Choose all that apply.)**
   a. A
   b. MX
   c. NS
   d. SOA
4. **What is the new type of DNS record for Windows 2000 domain controllers?**
   a. CNAME
   b. DC
   c. SRV
   d. SVR
5. **A DNS server can act as a DHCP client.**
   a. True
   b. False
6. **When running Dynamic DNS, which computers may register their A and PTR records? (Choose all that apply.)**
   a. Windows 2000 domain controllers
   b. Windows 2000 member servers
   c. Windows 2000 Professional machines
   d. Windows 2000 NT Workstation machines
7. **What is required to have redundancy within your DNS namespace?**
   a. Primary zone server
   b. Caching server
   c. Secondary zone server
   d. Reverse lookup zone server

OBJECTIVES

2.2 Configure network services for interoperability

NETWORK SERVICES • DHCP • DNS • WINS

UNDERSTANDING THE OBJECTIVE

The DHCP service automates client TCP/IP configuration. The DNS service provides host name-to-IP address resolution. Use the WINS service if earlier versions of Microsoft Windows are present or you want NetBIOS name-to-IP address mappings for legacy applications.

WHAT YOU REALLY NEED TO KNOW

- Four phases are involved in leasing an IP address from a DHCP server: DHCDISCOVER, DHCOFFER, DHCPREQUEST, and DHCPACK.
- The client attempts to renew its IP address lease, when appropriate. If the client does not renew its lease at 87.5% of the lease interval, the client broadcasts to any available server.
- The DHCP service provides IP addresses and subnet masks. Other common options are DNS, WINS, and default gateway configurations made through the DHCP manager.
- Three DNS zone types exist: Active Directory-integrated, standard primary, and standard secondary.
- Use only the following characters for domain names: A to Z (lowercase or uppercase) and the hyphen (-).
- Reverse lookups use the in-addr.arpa.dns suffix. When implementing a WINS server, configure DHCP to use the H-node for the node type. This choice forces clients to query the WINS server before performing a broadcast.
- WINS push replication is based on the number of changes to the database; pull replication is based on the time of day.

OBJECTIVES ON THE JOB

Many new features in Windows 2000, such as RIS installations, require the use of DHCP. DHCP also allows you to give clients the address for the WINS server, the DNS server, and the default gateway. The DNS server is necessary for accessing the Internet. WINS is necessary to support down-level clients and NetBIOS applications. You can also reduce network broadcasts by using WINS.

PRACTICE TEST QUESTIONS

1. **When multiple DHCP servers exist, which server provides clients with an IP address?**
   a. The last server contacted
   b. The nearest server
   c. The first server to respond
   d. The server that acts as the master browser
2. **Which options must be selected when defining a WINS server in DHCP? (Choose all that apply.)**
   a. 12/ WINS Computer Name
   b. 15/ Domain Name
   c. 44/ WINS Server
   d. 46/ NetBIOS Node type
3. **Which file can reside on clients and provide NetBIOS-to-IP address resolution?**
   a. HOST.TXT
   b. HOSTS.TXT
   c. LMHOSTS.TXT
   d. LMHOSTS
4. **Which machines may act as DHCP clients? (Choose all that apply.)**
   a. DNS servers
   b. Domain controllers
   c. Windows 2000 Professional machines
   d. Windows 95 machines
5. **What is required to reserve a client address?**
   a. A client's computer name
   b. A client's IP address
   c. A client's MAC address
   d. A domain name
6. **What is the final process used by the server to remove records from WINS?**
   a. Releasing
   b. Tombstoning
   c. Scavenging
   d. Deleting
7. **Which command shows the DNS server's IP address bound to your NIC?**
   a. DNSLOOKUP
   b. NSLOOKUP
   c. IPCONFIG
   d. IPCONFIG /ALL

OBJECTIVES

2.3 Configure access to printers

CONFIGURE PRINTERS • PRINT DEVICE

UNDERSTANDING THE OBJECTIVE

The first step in setting up printers or a printer pool is to configure the printers. After configuring the printer, you will need to set permissions and manage your printers. Windows 2000 Server can take advantage of the Internet Printing Protocol to manage and print documents over the Internet or an intranet.

WHAT YOU REALLY NEED TO KNOW

- Microsoft defines a printer as the software interface. It considers the physical machine to be the print device.
- Both Windows 2000 Server and Professional may act as print servers.
- Windows 2000 Professional is limited to 10 concurrent connections.
- Adequate hard disk space is essential on all print servers. Spooled print jobs may be larger than the actual data read by the print application.
- Print service for UNIX must be installed to print to a UNIX printer.
- Use priorities to control the order in which documents are printed. The highest priority is 99; the lowest is 1.
- To use Internet printing, **IIS** or **PWS** must be installed on the print server.

OBJECTIVES ON THE JOB

When configuring printers, you must decide whether the device will be a network printer or local printer, and whether to share it. If it is shared, you must select the appropriate printer priority settings. If you plan to use **IPP**, IIS or PWS must be installed on the print server. To access printers over the Internet, you must have Internet Explorer 4.x or later.

PRACTICE TEST QUESTIONS

1. **When a printer is installed on a Windows 2000 print server, which printer drivers are installed? (Choose all that apply).**
    a. Windows 2000
    b. Windows NT 4.0
    c. Windows 98
    d. Windows 95
    e. Windows for Workgroups 3.11
2. **What are the default permissions when you share a printer? (Choose all that apply.)**
    a. Everyone Print
    b. Everyone Manage Documents
    c. Everyone Full Control
    d. Administrators Full Control
3. **Which port do you use to print to a UNIX printer?**
    a. LPT1
    b. COM1
    c. LPR
    d. DLC
4. **When setting up print pools, all of the print devices must be the same.**
    a. True
    b. False
5. **When setting up print pools, all of the printer drivers must be the same.**
    a. True
    b. False
6. **Which service must be installed on a Windows 2000 Professional printer server using IPP?**
    a. IIS
    b. PWS
    c. TCP/IP printing
    d. Internet Connection Sharing
7. **How can you make the list of printers searchable?**
    a. Enable sharing
    b. Publish them in DNS
    c. Publish them in Active Directory
    d. Publish them in IIS

OBJECTIVES

2.4 Control access to printers

PRINTER PERMISSIONS • SHARING

UNDERSTANDING THE OBJECTIVE

You must thoroughly understand the factors and methods involved in controlling access to printers and the benefits of publishing printers in Active Directory. In addition, you should understand how the Internet Printing Protocol works. You should also know the details of assigning security permissions to users and groups as well as configuring printer pooling, assigning priorities, and scheduling print times.

WHAT YOU REALLY NEED TO KNOW

- Printer permissions consist of Print, Manage Documents, and Manage Printers. The default permission is Everyone Print.
- All print jobs—but not specific documents—on a faulty printer may be redirected to another printer, provided it uses the same print driver.
- When publishing printers to Active Directory, fill in the location and comment boxes, as a user will be searching for this information.
- Gain access to printers either through the Printers folder or through the Active Directory Users and Computers snap-in.
- Assign high priorities (99 is the highest) to printers of critical documents.
- Schedule print times for large jobs when the printers are not busy.
- Manage printers via a Web browser at either *http://<print-server>/printers* or *http://<print-server>/<printer shared name>*.
- You can publish printers running on Windows NT 4.0 or 3.51 in Active Directory.

OBJECTIVES ON THE JOB

When configuring printers, the default permission is the Everyone Print permission. You can manage printers through the printer folder in the Control Panel, by using the search feature in Active Directory Users and Computers, or possibly via a Web browser. IIS or PWS must be installed before you can use a Web browser to manage your printers. If a print device malfunctions, you can redirect all print jobs to another port and continue printing. The devices need not be the same, but the print drivers must be identical. Use priorities to control print jobs assigned to the more critical staff members. Use scheduling to print large print jobs during off-peak hours.

PRACTICE TEST QUESTIONS

The following users and groups exist on the Windows 2000 domain, images.com:

Administrators: Abby and Alex

Managers: Marion, Maxwell, and Melissa

Personnel: Pete and Phyllis

Printer 1 has all groups configured with Print permission except the Administrators group, which has Manage Printers permission.

Printer 2 has the default permissions.

Printer 3 is for the personnel department only and is configured with the Personnel group, Manage Documents, and Everyone Deny Print settings.

All three printers are published in Active Directory and are the same type of print device.

1. **Printer 1 has a problem and Marion has a document in the queue. As the administrator, you attempt to redirect her document to Printer 2, but your effort fails. Why can't her document be redirected?**
   a. The Managers group does not have Print permission.
   b. The Administrator does not have Full Control on Printer 1.
   c. The Administrator has only Print permission on Printer 2.
   d. Single documents may not be redirected.
2. **Pete tries to print payroll documents to Printer 3, but is unable to print. Why can't he print?**
   a. Manage Documents does not include the Print permission.
   b. A group policy prevents him from printing.
   c. The Administrator has only Print permission on Printer 2.
   d. Single documents may not be redirected.
3. **Company policy dictates that any document printed by the Managers group should print before other documents. This prioritization has not been happening. What is the best solution to this problem?**
   a. Create another printer on print device Printer 1 called MgrPrntr. Assign MgrPrntr a priority of 1 and assign Printer 1 a priority of 99. Tell all users other than managers to print to Printer 1 and inform the managers to print to MgrPrntr.
   b. Create another printer on print device Printer 1 called MgrPrntr. Assign MgrPrntr a priority of 99 and assign Printer 1 a priority of 1. Tell all users other than managers to print to Printer 1 and inform the managers to print to MgrPrntr.
   c. Assign the Managers group a priority of 1 on Printer 1, and assign all other groups a priority of 99.
   d. Assign the Managers group a priority of 99 on Printer 1, and assign all other groups a priority of 1.

OBJECTIVES

2.5 Monitor access to printers

MONITOR • PRINTER • AUDITING

UNDERSTANDING THE OBJECTIVE

You must understand the steps necessary to enable auditing and be able to configure auditing on printers. In addition, you must understand the ways in which local and group policies affect auditing; the different choices you can make, and reasons you should make those choices. You should also be able to access the audit logs and filter based on printer events.

WHAT YOU REALLY NEED TO KNOW

- ◆ On Windows 2000 Professional, you must set up the Local Audit policy first.
- ◆ On Windows 2000 Server, you must use the Group Policy snap-in to enable auditing.
- ◆ When monitoring printers, enable the Audit Object Access option for both successful and failed events.
- ◆ Configure specific printer options after enabling auditing by opening the properties of the designed printer and clicking the Advanced button on the Security tab.
- ◆ To audit files and folders, you must be logged on as a member of the Administrators group or have been granted the Manage auditing and security log right in Group Policy.
- ◆ In the Event Log, you can filter on the event source, category, event ID, user, computer, or date range to help isolate suspected problems.

OBJECTIVES ON THE JOB

You must be an Administrator or a user who has been granted the rights to manage auditing through Group Policy to audit and view security logs. When monitoring access to printers, make sure the local or group policy is set to enable Object Access. The next step is to define the levels of auditing for the selected users and groups. Auditing printers may result in extremely large log files; use the filtering option to refine your search of audit events.

PRACTICE TEST QUESTIONS

1. **When setting up the audit policy, which policy allows you to monitor printers?**
    a. Audit Object Access
    b. Audit Object Events
    c. Audit Printer Access
    d. Audit Systems Events
2. **When setting up auditing on Windows 2000 Professional when the operating system is acting as a printer server, what is the first step in auditing printers?**
    a. Define the events in the individual printer you want audited
    b. Define the groups you want monitored on the individual printer
    c. Enable the proper audit policy in Group Policy
    d. Enable the proper audit policy in the local policy
3. **On which items can you filter in the security log? (Choose all that apply.)**
    a. Computer
    b. Printer ID
    c. Printer name
    d. User
4. **Who can set up auditing?**
    a. Only Administrators
    b. Power Users
    c. Any user or group with the Manage Printers permission
    d. Everyone
5. **Every Monday, the permissions on a printer pool are changed from those used on Friday evening. What should you do to troubleshoot the problem?**
    a. Audit Change Permissions on the printer for the Everyone group
    b. Audit Change Permissions on the printer for the Administrators group
    c. Audit Manage Printers on the printer for the Everyone group
    d. Audit Policy Change on the printer for the Everyone group
6. **Which users or groups can view security logs? (Choose all that apply.)**
    a. Only the Administrator account
    b. Any user in the Administrators group
    c. Any user in the Power Users or Administrators group on a Windows 2000 server
    d. Any user with the View Security Logs permission configured in Group Policy
7. **Where can the audit option be found on the printer properties sheet?**
    a. Advanced tab
    b. General tab
    c. Security tab
    d. Sharing tab

OBJECTIVES

2.6 Troubleshoot access to printers

TROUBLESHOOT • PRINTERS

UNDERSTANDING THE OBJECTIVE

Many different problems can arise, in a variety of circumstances, while troubleshooting printers—for example, while troubleshooting Windows 2000 Professional or Server print servers, a Web server, or client computers. The problems can range from network connectivity issues to Group Policy problems to hardware failure. Understanding what to look for and how system requirements come into play is critical.

WHAT YOU REALLY NEED TO KNOW

- A lack of hard drive space for the spool folder may keep documents from printing.
- Garbled text on a printed document usually indicates use of the wrong printer driver.
- Denied Access messages almost always correspond to incorrectly assigned permissions.
- Not all printers in a printer pool that print improperly are different or use different print drivers than those functioning properly.
- Scheduling of print jobs or changing the default priority of 1 may have unexpected consequences.
- All versions of Windows 2000 have IPP printing support, and this feature is available as an add-on for Microsoft Windows 95 and Microsoft Windows 98 clients.
- Internet Explorer 4.01 or later is required to view the printer page.
- To create an LPR port and then print to a UNIX printer, you must choose a local printer and Print Services for UNIX must be installed.
- When a print device fails, you may redirect all print jobs to another printer that uses the same print driver.

OBJECTIVES ON THE JOB

To create and administer a printer on Windows 2000 Server, you must be a member of the Administrators or Power Users group. Understanding the unique symptoms of printer problems can lead to their quick resolution. Administration of print servers can be accomplished in three ways: through the printer folder in the Control Panel, via a Web browser, or through Active Directory.

PRACTICE TEST QUESTIONS

1. **When scanning the Event Log, you notice that your disk space on the C: drive is getting low. Drive D: has almost 5 GB free. When the print server was set up, space was not an issue. How can you solve this problem now?**
   a. For each printer installed, redirect the spooler folder to the D: drive.
   b. For the print server, redirect the spooler folder to the D: drive.
   c. Copy and paste the C:\WINNT\System32\spool\PRINTERS to the D: drive.
   d. Reinstall the print server and set D:\spool\PRINTERS as the spool folder.

2. **Your print server is a Windows 2000 Server. Your client machines are Windows NT 4.0 clients. You try connecting to a printer via the Web but fail. What is most likely causing this problem?**
   a. IIS is not installed on the server.
   b. PWS is not installed on the workstation.
   c. TCP/IP is not bound to the workstation NIC.
   d. The browser is Internet Explorer 3.x.

3. **A user attempts to print to a new printer outside his office and receives the message "Access Denied." You have verified that the primary group to which he belongs has Print permission. What might cause this problem?**
   a. The printer is configured to print between 10 p.m. and 4 a.m.
   b. The printer priority is set to 0.
   c. Another group to which the user belongs to has Deny Print permission.
   d. The printer driver was never installed.

4. **A single document can be redirected to another printer.**
   a. True
   b. False

5. **How much hard drive space should be allocated to print simple documents?**
   a. 2 MB
   b. 8 MB
   c. 32 MB
   d. 64 MB

6. **When searching for the first-floor color printer in Active Directory, you cannot find any located on that floor. What is most likely the cause of this problem?**
   a. You do not have permission to search Active Directory.
   b. The print server is on a Windows NT 4.0 server.
   c. The location field was left blank.
   d. The printer was installed on a Windows 2000 member server.

OBJECTIVES

2.7 Configure access to files, folders, and shared folders

FILES • FOLDERS • SHARES • SHARE-LEVEL ACCESS • PERMISSIONS

UNDERSTANDING THE OBJECTIVE

You must understand how to create folders and shares, NTFS permissions, and effective permissions. In addition, you must know which administrative shares exist on a Windows 2000 computer. You must also understand how to hide a share as well as how moving and copying files from partitions affects permissions.

WHAT YOU REALLY NEED TO KNOW

- Remove the Everyone group and add the Administrators group to most folders.
- The default permissions for both shares and NTFS are Everyone—Full Control.
- Create shares from the server or through the Computer Management utility.
- Share permissions are intended for folders only; they cannot be applied to individual files.
- When you copy or move files between or within partitions, those files inherit the permissions of the destination folder. The exception occurs when you move files within a partition; in that case, the permissions are retained.
- NTFS permissions may be applied to files and folders. They work together with share permissions to provide for effective permissions.
- Deny—Full Control overrides all other permissions.
- Configure Home folders on an NTFS permission on a server where the files can be marked for backups. You can accomplish this task through the Active Directory Users and Groups.
- Give users only Read and Execute permissions on application folders to prevent them from deleting important files.
- You can use group policies to change the target folder location of any user's My Documents folder.

OBJECTIVES ON THE JOB

FAT partitions have only share-level security. NTFS permissions add another level of granular control at the file or folder level. When configuring folder permissions, you must decide whether to allow inheritance. To hide shares, use the $ sign. To control local access, use NTFS permissions. The following administrative shares exist upon installation: the root of each volume; C$, D$, and so on; ADMIN$ and PRINT$ when the first printer is shared. SYSVOL is a share that is created to replace the NETLOGON directory from Windows NT 4.0.

PRACTICE TEST QUESTIONS

1. **By default, which groups or users have some level of control on a new share?**
   a. Creator/Owner
   b. Administrators group
   c. Administrator account
   d. Everyone group
2. **What is the NTFS permission that is similar to the Change share permission?**
   a. Change
   b. Read/write
   c. Modify
   d. Overwrite
3. **On which tab in a user's properties sheet do you define the location of the Home folder?**
   a. Remote Control tab
   b. Environment tab
   c. Profile tab
   d. Account tab
4. **In which directory in a user's properties sheet do you define the location of the Home folder?**
   a. \\ABC\users\%username%
   b. \\ABC\users/%username%
   c. \\ABC\home\%username%
   d. \\ABC\home/%username%
5. **A group has Change share permissions for a particular folder but is not listed under the NTFS permissions. This group needs to run applications from that folder. Which NTFS permissions do the group members need? (Choose all that apply.)**
   a. Read
   b. List
   c. Execute
   d. Run As
6. **Which of the following shares that exist on computer ABC are available to any user on your domain if the default permissions are assigned? (Choose all that apply.)**
   a. C$
   b. ADMIN$
   c. AMDIN
   d. PRINTER$

OBJECTIVES

2.8 Control access to files, folders, and shared resources

FILES • FOLDERS • SHARES • SHARE-LEVEL ACCESS • PERMISSIONS • NTFS

UNDERSTANDING THE OBJECTIVE

You must understand inheritance, including how to block it. Also, you must know how to combine share-level permissions and NTFS permissions and how to use the advanced permissions on NTFS partitions. You must understand how Deny—Full Control affects permissions. Share-level permissions cannot apply to individual files, so you should be aware of the requirements associated with their use.

WHAT YOU REALLY NEED TO KNOW

- In addition to administrative shares for each partition (that is, C$ and D$), ADMIN$ and PRINT$ administrative shares exist in Windows 2000.
- ADMIN$ maps to the system root, typically C:\WINNT.
- PRINT$ maps to the systemroot\system32\spool\drivers folder.
- To prevent permissions from being propagated to subdirectories, clear the check box to allow inheritance on NTFS permissions only. This option does not exist for shares.
- Effective permissions are created when you choose the most restrictive option between the cumulative share permissions and the cumulative NTFS permissions.
- Deny—Full Control overrides any other permissions.
- Advanced permissions allow you to exert more granular control over NTFS permissions.
- Encryption can be used only on noncompressed, NTFS volumes.
- When you change a user's permissions, that person must log off, then log back on to receive the new permissions.

OBJECTIVES ON THE JOB

Only Administrators, Power Users, and Server operators can share folders. When creating shares, you should assign the most restrictive permissions available to groups when possible, and to users when necessary. Remove the Everyone group. Use Authenticated Users if every person on the domain should have access. You can control access to shares by limiting the connections.

PRACTICE TEST QUESTIONS

The xyz.com domain has a server called fileserv, on which all volumes are formatted with NTFS. The following shares exist: Southeast, Florida, Georgia, Alabama, South Carolina, and Louisiana. The individual state shares are subdirectories of the Southeast folder.

The Managers group has Full Control on the Southeast share as well as Full Control, NTFS permissions. The Flmanagers group has Change permissions on the share for Florida and Read, Write and Execute, NTFS permissions. Every state manager has corresponding permissions on his or her own state folder.

1. **Sarah, a member of the Managers group, accesses reports from the Florida share. What will be her effective permissions?**
   a. Read/Execute
   b. Write
   c. Change
   d. Full Control
2. **Sarah accesses the Florida folder through the Southeast share. What will be her effective permissions?**
   a. Read/Execute
   b. Write
   c. Change
   d. Full Control
3. **Sarah accesses the Alabama folder locally. What will be her permissions?**
   a. Change
   b. Modify
   c. Full Control
   d. No Access
4. **The president of the company wants David, a member of the Almanagers group, to have access to all files and folders. Sarah adds his user account to the Southeast share with Change permissions. Which folders can David now access?**
   a. Southeast
   b. Alabama
   c. Southeast, Florida, Georgia, Alabama, South Carolina, Louisiana
   d. None of the folders
5. **You decide to stop sharing the individual state folders and give the Everyone group Full Control over the Southeast share. Which folders can Debbie, a member of the Gamanagers group, now access?**
   a. Southeast
   b. Georgia
   c. Southeast, Florida, Georgia, Alabama, South Carolina, Louisiana
   d. None of the folders

OBJECTIVES

2.9 Monitor access to files, folders, and shared folders

FILES • FOLDERS • SHARES • AUDITING • SHARED FOLDER UTILITY

UNDERSTANDING THE OBJECTIVE

You must understand the steps necessary to enable auditing. In particular, you should be able to configure auditing on files, folders, and shares. Also, you must understand how local and group policies affect auditing, which choices you can make, and why you should make them. You should be able to use the Shared Folder utility to view user sessions and list which files are currently open.

WHAT YOU REALLY NEED TO KNOW

- On Windows 2000 Professional, you must set up the Local Audit policy first.
- On a Windows 2000 Server, you must use the Group Policy snap-in to enable auditing.
- When auditing files and folders, you must determine which type of events to enable in the Audit Object Access option—successful and/or failed events.
- To see which users currently have sessions open to the machine, view the Sessions folder in the Shared Folder utility within the Computer Management utility.
- To see which files are currently open, view the Open Files folder in the Shared Folder utility.
- To audit files and folders, you must be logged on as a member of the Administrators group or have been granted the Manage auditing and security log right in Group Policy.
- You can audit only on NTFS partitions.

OBJECTIVES ON THE JOB

You must be an Administrator or a user who has been granted the rights to manage auditing through Group Policy before you can audit and view security logs. When monitoring access to files and folders, make sure the Local Audit or Group Policy is set to enable object access. The next step is to define the level of auditing desired for the selected users and groups. You can monitor, in real time, which files are open or which users have sessions open on a computer through the Shared Folder utility.

PRACTICE TEST QUESTIONS

1. **What information is included in the security log? (Choose all that apply.)**
   a. The action performed
   b. The user who performed an action
   c. The success or failure of an action
   d. The domain to which the user is logged in
2. **Files and folders on FAT32 volumes can be audited.**
   a. True
   b. False
3. **From a command prompt, what can you type to update an audit policy?**
   a. AUDIT/REFRESHPOLICY
   b. AUDIT /UPDATEPOLICY
   c. SECEDIT /REFRESHPOLICY
   d. SECEDIT /UPDATEPOLICY
4. **You want to open an Access database in exclusive mode, but are told that the file is in use. How can you find out which user has the file open?**
   a. Click In Use on the properties sheet of the machine from Server Manager
   b. Double-click Shares from Server Manager
   c. Click Sessions in the Shared Folder utility
   d. Click Open Files in the Shared Folder utility
5. **If you are not an Administrator, which right will allow you to view the security log?**
   a. Access this computer from the network
   b. Create shared objects
   c. Manage security logs
   d. Manage auditing and security logs
6. **Disconnecting users from shares may cause data loss.**
   a. True
   b. False
7. **When you try to access the administrative share PRINT$, an error message states that the network path could not be found. What would cause such an error?**
   a. The administrative share is actually PRINTER$.
   b. The administrative share is actually PRINTERS$.
   c. No printers exist in the printer folder.
   d. No printer is shared in the printer folder.

OBJECTIVES

2.10 Troubleshoot access to files, folders, and shared folders

FILES • FOLDERS • SHARES • NTFS • TROUBLESHOOT

UNDERSTANDING THE OBJECTIVE

File access permissions vary between local (NTFS) and network (share) access to files and folders. When accessing NTFS files or directories through a share, calculating effective permissions means choosing the more restrictive options among the applicable share permissions and NTFS permissions. For each individual type of permission (share or NTFS), identifying effective permissions requires assessing all applicable permissions across the account and related group memberships. Because users get permissions in the form of an access token supplied at login, changing a user's or group's permissions requires that the user or group member log off and then back on to make the changes effective.

WHAT YOU REALLY NEED TO KNOW

- Share permissions and NFTS permissions are cumulative except when Deny—Full Control is selected; this choice overrides all other permissions.
- Deny—Full Control is the Windows NT 4.0 equivalent of No Access.
- Be careful when setting up shares within folders that are already shared.
- Deselecting permissions is not the same as denying permissions. By clearing all check boxes, you essentially remove the group from the permissions list.
- When users log on locally, share permissions do not apply.
- When a user who has encrypted a file leaves the company, the person who holds the recovery agent can decrypt the file.
- The Modify permission in NTFS replaces the Windows NT 4.0 Change permission.
- Giving a user Read, Write, and Execute permissions does not automatically extend the Delete permission to that individual; however, all data in a file may be deleted.
- NTFS permissions cannot be assigned to FAT or FAT32 volumes.
- The only groups that may share folders are Administrators, Server Operators, and Power Users.

OBJECTIVES ON THE JOB

Consider using NTFS whenever possible, as it allows for more granular control. In addition, it supports compression and encryption, albeit not at the same time. Also, consider giving the Everyone group the default permissions and controlling access via the NTFS permissions on the files and folders. This approach makes troubleshooting permission problems much easier.

PRACTICE TEST QUESTIONS

You have a Windows 2000 Server with three partitions: C:, D:, and E:. The C: and D: partitions are formatted with NTFS; the E: drive is formatted with FAT32. There is 100 MB free on the C: partition, which is where the system and boot files are installed. There is 2 GB free on each of the D: and E: partitions. All of the folders on each of the D: partition are compressed. On the D: drive, you have the default permissions for all of the shares. NTFS permissions control access to these files.

1. **You have a file that is encrypted on the C: drive. You understand that moving encrypted files between NTFS partitions retains their encryption status. Upon viewing the attributes on the file while it resides on the D: drive, you find it is _______.**
   a. encrypted
   b. compressed
   c. compressed and encrypted
   d. You receive an error message when attempting to move the file
2. **You have a folder called Contracts on the D: partition. The Lawyers group is constantly modifying or adding important contracts to this folder. In the process, files are sometimes accidentally deleted. Which NTFS permission must you select to allow the Lawyers group to continue functioning, but prevent group members from deleting the files? (Choose all that apply.)**
   a. Full Control
   b. Modify
   c. Read and Execute
   d. Read
   e. Write
3. **If you move the Contracts folder to the E: partition, who will be able to access the files and with what permissions?**
   a. No one; the Everyone—Deny All permission is selected
   b. Everyone—Full Control
   c. Creator/Owner
   d. The Lawyers group—Modify permissions
4. **You have a 70 MB file on the D: partition that you attempt to copy to the C: partition. The operation fails. Why?**
   a. You must be an Administrator to copy files across partitions.
   b. Compressed files cannot be moved to noncompressed partitions.
   c. The uncompressed file size exceeds 100 MB.
   d. The paging file needs room to grow.
5. **The paging file should be placed on which partition?**
   a. C:
   b. D:
   c. E:

OBJECTIVES

2.11 Configure a stand-alone Distributed File System (Dfs)

STAND-ALONE • DISTRIBUTED FILE SYSTEM (DFS)

UNDERSTANDING THE OBJECTIVE

You must know the limitations that apply stand-alone Dfs roots as well as their benefits. In particular, you must understand how permissions are handled for stand-alone Dfs roots, which file systems you can use, and which you should choose. You should also understand the client requirements when integrating them with Dfs (and identify those clients that cannot use Dfs). In addition, you must know how many Dfs roots you can establish on any server and for any domain.

WHAT YOU REALLY NEED TO KNOW

- Stand-alone Dfs roots may be located on any file system.
- Stand-alone Dfs cannot use Active Directory.
- Stand-alone Dfs roots do not support replication.
- Dfs permissions are handled through share permissions. If a stand-alone Dfs root resides on an NTFS partition, it obtains effective access permissions just like a share.
- The three parts of a Dfs are its root, its link, and its shared folders.
- To use Dfs with down-level clients, you must add the Dfs Service for Microsoft Clients to each machine.
- Windows 3.11 and earlier cannot take advantage of Dfs.
- Shares that act as Dfs links may reside on multiple network hosts, yet function as a single logical file system.
- You may create a stand-alone Dfs root by using FAT, FAT32, or NTFS. You can add access controls only when using NTFS, however.
- Stand-alone servers do not support replication or multiple levels in their roots.
- Windows 95, Windows 98, Windows NT, and Windows 2000 can all access a Dfs root, but down-level clients require the installation of a special Dfs client to do so.

OBJECTIVES ON THE JOB

Dfs is a welcome feature in Windows 2000. It allows you to link to all shares, yet makes it appear as though every folder resides in a single location. This feature makes life easier for the end user and ultimately for Administrators as well. Utilize hidden shares to prevent users from seeing the actual underlying share.

PRACTICE TEST QUESTIONS

1. **What do you call the server that contains the Dfs root?**
    a. Root server
    b. File server
    c. Host server
    d. DFS server
2. **When creating the Dfs root, you must use an existing share as the Dfs root share.**
    a. True
    b. False
3. **How many Dfs links may be assigned to a Dfs root?**
    a. 1
    b. 100
    c. 1000
    d. Unlimited
4. **The Dfs service is auto-installed with Windows 2000 Server.**
    a. True
    b. False
5. **After selecting the share that will act as an additional stand-alone Dfs link, what else must you select?**
    a. Group permissions
    b. Link name
    c. Comment field
    d. Creator/Owner
6. **To hide shares but make them visible in the Dfs root, what must you do?**
    a. Use %<sharename>% on the original share
    b. Use $ after the share name
    c. Use & after the share name
    d. Not possible—shares will remain hidden in the Dfs root
7. **How many domain controllers may host the same Dfs root?**
    a. 2
    b. 8
    c. 16
    d. 32

OBJECTIVES

2.12 Manage a stand-alone Distributed File System

STAND-ALONE • DISTRIBUTED FILE SYSTEM (DFS)

UNDERSTANDING THE OBJECTIVE

You must be able to assign permissions to shares in Dfs links. You must also understand how to manage access controls to these files. With stand-alone Dfs roots, you may use only one root and one level of shares or links under that single root.

WHAT YOU REALLY NEED TO KNOW

- Only shared folders may be used as Dfs links.
- The permissions assigned to Dfs links match those assigned to the underlying share. You cannot handle permissions through Dfs.
- You can use the FAT, FAT32, or NTFS file systems when creating stand-alone Dfs roots.
- Carefully consider how a partition is formatted when setting permissions. The best access controls are available when NTFS is used to format a partition that contains a stand-alone Dfs root.
- Stand-alone Dfs roots contain one root folder, which may be an existing share or a new root folder created through the Dfs Wizard.
- Stand-alone Dfs roots are not published to Active Directory. As a consequence, they are not searchable in Active Directory.
- Replication is not available for stand-alone roots.
- The Dfs service is part of the operating system, so it cannot be uninstalled.
- You can adjust the length of time during which clients cache their Dfs link referrals.

OBJECTIVES ON THE JOB

Managing Dfs roots and links is quite simple. The most difficult point is to remember which permissions apply to the underlying shared folders. If you have established a well-designed shared folder system with solid permissions, this task simply requires setting up an initial Dfs root and creating Dfs links. Domain-based Dfs roots are preferred to stand-alone Dfs roots for reasons discussed in later sections of this book. Consider using NTFS partitions for the same reason you would use them when setting up shares—namely, to exploit NTFS's ability to impose access controls on individual files and directories and to exert more granular control over files and directories in the resulting Dfs environment.

PRACTICE TEST QUESTIONS

1. **The Dfs service can be uninstalled from Windows 2000 server.**
    a. True
    b. False
2. **Which of the following can be done from the stand-alone Dfs module?**
    a. Create a single-level structure
    b. Create multiple single-level structures
    c. Alter share permissions
    d. Publish Dfs links to Active Directory
3. **The shared folder permissions are __________________.**
    a. overridden by Dfs permissions
    b. determined by the permissions of the Dfs root
    c. left intact
    d. determined by the Administrator using the Dfs Link Wizard.
4. **All folders on the Windows 2000 server can become Dfs links.**
    a. True
    b. False
5. **A Windows 95 machine cannot see the Dfs root. How can this problem be solved?**
    a. Install Dfs Services for Microsoft Networks
    b. Install Dfs Services for Windows 2000
    c. Install Dfs Services for Windows 95
    d. Install Dfs Services for Windows 2000 Professional
6. **You decided to remove a Dfs link, but some users remain able to use the link. Why do some machines continue to store this information?**
    a. It remains on the client until the user logs off.
    b. It persists until the machine is rebooted.
    c. It was cached and the cache time has not elapsed.
    d. You did not commit the changes.
7. **You try, but fail, to add a second Dfs root to the stand-alone Dfs root. Why?**
    a. Only one Dfs root is allowed per server.
    b. A local security policy allows only one Dfs root on that machine.
    c. A domain security policy allows only one Dfs root on that machine.
    d. A GPO has been linked to all Dfs roots, preventing multiple roots.

OBJECTIVES

2.13 Troubleshoot Distributed File System (Dfs)

TROUBLESHOOT DISTRIBUTED FILE SYSTEM • DFS • DOMAIN AND STAND-ALONE

UNDERSTANDING THE OBJECTIVE

It is important that you be able to identify problems that arise during and after Dfs setup, both for stand-alone and domain-based roots. Stand-alone Dfs servers represent a single point of failure; thus, if a Dfs server is offline, so are all of its Dfs shares (links). You must understand how to verify that a Dfs link is properly configured and accessible to its target users. Effective permissions control access to files on NTFS partitions, whereas share permissions control access to FAT and FAT32 partitions. If users cannot access their folders but see a Dfs link, it usually indicates a permission problem of some kind. You should configure whatever Dfs cache referral time is appropriate for your clients and your networking environment.

WHAT YOU REALLY NEED TO KNOW

- Replication may occur only when the Dfs root on a server has been formatted using NTFS version 5.0.
- Use the Check Status option to verify that a Dfs share is properly configured and accessible.
- Share permissions control access to Dfs links.
- Windows 95, Windows 98, and Windows NT workstations must install the Dfs Services for Microsoft Clients to access any Dfs root.
- You cannot delete a share that is configured as a Dfs link, unless you first delete that Dfs link.
- Only one Dfs root can exist for any given server.
- You cannot publish a Dfs topology to Active Directory on a stand-alone Dfs server.

OBJECTIVES ON THE JOB

Properly configuring your Dfs server at setup helps avoid potential problems. Microsoft makes two recommendations regarding Dfs. First, you should install Dfs roots on NTFS version 5.0 partitions. Second, you should choose domain-based Dfs over stand-alone Dfs roots, whenever possible. By following these two recommendations, you will be able to replicate your Dfs roots and enable basic fault-tolerance and load-balancing capabilities. For down-level clients, you must install the Dfs Services for Microsoft Clients on those machines. You must also know which permissions apply to target shares before you set up Dfs links to those shares, as those permissions govern access to them. On networks with volatile shares (lots of changes occur routinely), decrease the cache referral time to 30 minutes for such shares.

PRACTICE TEST QUESTIONS

1. **You are deleting old folders on the network and receive an error message indicating that a file is in use. You checked the Shared Folder utility and found that no one has the file open. Why can't this folder be deleted?**
    a. A user has accessed the folder through Dfs and the file is in use.
    b. You cannot delete a shared folder that is also a Dfs link until the link is removed.
    c. A user is accessing the file locally, which isn't shown in Open Files.
    d. Only the Enterprise Administrator may delete shared folders.
2. **A Dfs link points to a folder whose contents change frequently. What should you do to ensure that users will have a more accurate picture of the contents of the folder?**
    a. Increase the cache referral time for the Dfs link
    b. Decrease the cache referral time for the Dfs link
    c. Increase the Time to Live value
    d. Decrease the Time to Live value
3. **You want to create a Windows 2000 Dfs root replica to provide for redundancy and load balancing. Which factors would prevent you from using the feature? (Choose all that apply.)**
    a. The Dfs root is on an NTFS version 4.0 partition.
    b. The Dfs root is on an NTFS version 5.0 partition.
    c. The Dfs root is on a FAT32 partition.
    d. The Dfs root is on a stand-alone Dfs.
    e. The Dfs root is on a domain-based Dfs.
4. **You believe that a Dfs link is not pointing to a valid share. How can you quickly verify that a Dfs shared folder is configured and accessible?**
    a. Right-click the Dfs server and choose "Scan all links."
    b. Right-click the Dfs root and choose "Scan all links."
    c. Right-click the Dfs link and choose "Check status."
    d. Click the Dfs link, click Action, and then choose "Display Dfs link."
5. **You want to configure a new Dfs link. When you click Browse to find the share, you do not see the desired folder. What might cause this problem? (Choose all that apply.)**
    a. The folder is on a FAT16 partition.
    b. The folder is hidden.
    c. The folder is not shared.
    d. The folder has the share permission, Everyone—Deny—Full Control.
6. **You run a network consisting of mixed clients running Windows 2000 Professional and Windows 98. All Windows 2000 machines can access the Dfs shares, but none of the Windows 98 machines can see them. What must you do to allow the Windows 98 machines to access the Dfs shares?**
    a. Install DFS Services for Microsoft Clients on the Dfs root server
    b. Install DFS Services for Microsoft Clients on the Windows 98 machines
    c. Format the Windows 98 machines with NFTS version 5.0
    d. Switch the Windows 2000 Servers into mixed mode

OBJECTIVES

2.14 Configure a domain-based Dfs

DOMAIN-BASED • DISTRIBUTED FILE SYSTEM • DFS

UNDERSTANDING THE OBJECTIVE

You must understand the benefits that pertain to domain-based Dfs roots as well as the rules that apply to them. For example, you should know how permissions are handled for Dfs roots and which client requirements permit them to integrate with Dfs. You can establish only one root; you should also know how many roots are possible on a server for a domain. In addition, you must understand, and be able to configure, Dfs replication behavior.

WHAT YOU REALLY NEED TO KNOW

- The contents of the Dfs may be replicated to multiple servers.
- When shares are located across many servers but made available in a single location, users find it easier to locate information, and the network load is spread to the other servers.
- To create fault-tolerant Dfs roots, locate them exclusively on NTFS version 5.0 (or later) disk partitions.
- Replication does not occur on FAT or FAT32 volumes.
- A domain-based Dfs uses the FRS to automate file replication.
- When a shared folder is changed, the modification is replicated (at 15-minute intervals) to the server's replication partners.
- When setting up replication, you must select one share as the initial master share.
- You can control user access to the Dfs root, although this process is different from controlling access to shares. By default, Administrators are granted Full Control permission, and Authenticated Users are granted Read permission.

OBJECTIVES ON THE JOB

When you are setting up a domain-based Dfs server, it is strongly recommended that you locate the Dfs roots on NTFS partitions. Replication occurs only on NTFS partitions. NTFS permissions also support more granular control over Dfs links and shares. Although FRS is installed automatically, it is not configured automatically. To obtain the best results and highest availability, set FRS to replicate automatically. In addition to providing replication data for fault tolerance, because multiple clients can access data from multiple Dfs locations, this option enables server load balancing.

PRACTICE TEST QUESTIONS

1. **What is another name for domain-based Dfs?**
   a. Domain roots
   b. Fault-tolerant roots
   c. Replication roots
   d. Replica roots
2. **Windows NT 4.0 servers can be Dfs servers.**
   a. True
   b. False
3. **Replication can be set __________________. (Choose all that apply.)**
   a. to Manual
   b. to Scheduled
   c. to Automatic
   d. only on stand-alone servers
4. **What may be replicated? (Choose all that apply.)**
   a. A Dfs root
   b. A Dfs link
   c. A Dfs server
   d. A Dfs tree
5. **A domain-based Dfs must be placed on ____________. (Choose all that apply.)**
   a. a domain controller
   b. a member server
   c. a global catalog server only
   d. Windows 2000 Professional
6. **The File Replication Service is installed automatically during the Windows 2000 Server installation.**
   a. True
   b. False
7. **How often does intrasite replication occur?**
   a. Every 30 seconds
   b. Every 2 minutes
   c. Every 5 minutes
   d. Every 10 minutes
8. **Dfs replication is disabled by default.**
   a. True
   b. False

OBJECTIVES

2.15 Manage a domain-based Dfs

DOMAIN-BASED • DISTRIBUTED FILE SYSTEM • DFS • ROOTS

UNDERSTANDING THE OBJECTIVE

Only certain file systems may be used with Dfs, and you must understand the properties and advantages associated with each such file system (for stand-alone Dfs roots: FAT, FAT32, and NTFS; for domain-based roots: NTFS only). Understand that the **FRS** provides both data redundancy (multiple copies of data) and load balancing (simultaneous use of multiple copies of data).

WHAT YOU REALLY NEED TO KNOW

- Replication is available for domain-based Dfs roots.
- A domain-based root supports load balancing by replicating the root and making it available in multiple locations.
- Domain-based roots provide access to other redundant copies of data, when any one system with Dfs content goes offline.
- All Dfs information for domain-based roots is published to Active Directory.
- To use replication, you must format the partition when the Dfs root is installed as an NTFS file system.
- You do not need to assign permissions with Dfs. You do, however, need to know where the underlying shares reside, what permissions (if any) are associated with them, and in which file system they reside to determine their effective permissions.
- If you have multiple sites and want to use file replication, you must configure this option using the Active Directory Sites and Services snap-in.
- You must create at least one root replica before enabling replication.
- You may have multiple replicas.

OBJECTIVES ON THE JOB

You can manage your Dfs by using NTFS to create replicated Dfs roots. Creating a root replica is the first step in setting up replication. This task is accomplished in the Dfs snap-in within the MMC, through the Action menu. Just as you do when creating a new root, you can create a root replica on an existing share on another server or a new share specifically for that purpose. After you designate a root replica, set the first root as the master, then select a replica root and enable replication.

PRACTICE TEST QUESTIONS

1. **Only a Dfs root may be replicated.**
    a. True
    b. False
2. **Replication can occur only within a site.**
    a. True
    b. False
3. **To what does a Dfs-replicated link point?**
    a. Share folder
    b. Initial Dfs link
    c. Master Dfs link
    d. Dfs root
4. **Domain-based Dfs roots are automatically published to Active Directory.**
    a. True
    b. False
5. **How can you access the Dfs utility? (Choose all that apply.)**
    a. MMC snap-in
    b. Active Directory
    c. Administrative Tools
    d. Control Panel
6. **A server may have an unlimited number of roots.**
    a. True
    b. False
7. **A domain may have an unlimited number of roots.**
    a. True
    b. False

OBJECTIVES

2.16 Configure local security on files and folders

LOCAL SECURITY • NTFS PERMISSIONS

UNDERSTANDING THE OBJECTIVE

You must understand all three Windows 2000 file systems: FAT, FAT32, and NTFS. NTFS is the only file system that supports object-level security (individual access controls for volumes, files, and directories). You should understand that NTFS version 5.0 is incompatible with older versions of NTFS, and you should recognize the six basic permission types and how they're changed in Windows 2000. Permissions are cumulative, except when an explicit denial applies. Access denied always overrides any other permissions. By default, the Everyone group has Full Control over new volumes and directories.

WHAT YOU REALLY NEED TO KNOW

- If you are dual-booting Windows NT 4.0 Workstation and Windows 2000 Professional, for both operating systems to access files on all partitions, Windows NT 4.0 Workstation must have Service Pack 4 or higher applied.
- To use either **EFS** (encryption) or file compression within a disk partition, you must format that partition with NTFS.
- In Windows NT 4.0, to prevent any access, you select the No Access option. In Windows 2000, you prevent access by selecting Deny—Full Control unless you have a definite and specific reason.
- Because users or groups that are not granted explicit access to NTFS objects are denied access by default, another way to prevent unwanted access is to remove all user and group entries from the access control list for which you wish to deny access.
- FAT and FAT32 have no local security and thus no explicit controls over individual files and directories.
- By default, permissions are inherited by subfolders. They must be explicitly configured to prevent such inheritance.
- NTFS permissions are cumulative.

OBJECTIVES ON THE JOB

The benefits of having NTFS formatted partitions are substantial and such formatting should be used whenever possible. With NTFS, you can enable quotas, compression, and user encryption; have redundancy when using Dfs; and so on. It is strongly suggested that you remove Full Control permission from the Everyone group and replace it with the most restrictive permissions that allow users to complete their tasks. Whenever a user creates a file or folder, he or she becomes the Creator/Owner with Full Control. Do everything possible to control access with groups as opposed to users.

PRACTICE TEST QUESTIONS

A folder, Word, exists with the following groups and NTFS permissions assigned: Administrators—Full Control, Authenticated Users—Read, ExecAsst—Read and Write, Managers—Modify, and Wordproc—Read & Execute.

1. **Which group can run Winword.exe, which resides in the Word folder? (Choose all that apply.)**
   a. Administrators
   b. Authenticated Users
   c. ExecAsst
   d. Managers
   e. Wordproc
2. **What is the permission for a user who is in both the ExecAsst and Wordproc groups?**
   a. Read
   b. Read & Execute
   c. Read, Write, and Execute
   d. Modify
3. **Which group may delete files in the Word folder? (Choose all that apply.)**
   a. Administrators
   b. Authenticated Users
   c. ExecAsst
   d. Managers
   e. Wordproc
4. **The ExecAsst group can create new files and alter existing ones in the Word folder. Can this group also delete files?**
   a. Yes
   b. No
5. **You decide that the benefits of NTFS are so superior to those with FAT32 that you convert to NTFS. What are the NTFS permissions on all files and folders on the converted partition?**
   a. Everyone—Full Control
   b. Authenticated Users—Full Control
   c. Domain Users—Full Control
   d. Administrators—Full Control
6. **Which permission does Full Control have that Modify does not? (Choose all that apply.)**
   a. Delete
   b. Take Ownership
   c. Change Permissions
   d. Create New Folders

OBJECTIVES

2.17 Control local security on files and folders

CONTROL LOCAL SECURITY • NTFS PERMISSIONS

UNDERSTANDING THE OBJECTIVE

You must understand the basic and advanced NTFS permissions available on Windows 2000 servers. Any mention of local permissions means only NTFS permissions; share permissions do not come into play. You should understand how moving or copying files between partitions and file formats affects files. In addition, you should understand NTFS version 5.0's new inheritance mechanism and know how to prevent file inheritance when necessary. Disk quotas may also be used to limit disk access. To use disk quotas, you must format each partition on which you wish to monitor use with NTFS.

WHAT YOU REALLY NEED TO KNOW

- Six standard NTFS permissions exist. More granular controls are available through the Advanced option in the Security tab.
- When you copy data from any one NTFS partition to another, all copied files inherit the target folder's permissions.
- Moving files on the same NTFS partition retains their original permissions (because it moves only an NTFS file pointer in the file allocation table).
- The same rules that apply to NTFS permissions when copying and moving files also apply to file compression and Dfs.
- You may edit permissions only on a parent object. To alter permissions on a child object, you must first deselect the "Allow inheritable permissions parent to propagate to this object" box.
- When files are copied or moved to a FAT16 or FAT32 volume, all NTFS permissions are lost.

OBJECTIVES ON THE JOB

Permissions flow from the parent object to its children. If you wish to change any children without affecting the parent, you must block inheritance. In effect, this operation creates a new parent object. Moving and copying NTFS files causes them to inherit target folder permissions except when you move files within the same partition. NTFS permissions should be applied to groups whenever possible. To control disk usage, format partitions with NTFS and place disk quotas on user directories. When you change permissions, a user must log off and then log on again before those new permissions will become effective.

PRACTICE TEST QUESTIONS

You have a 15 GB hard drive partitioned as follows: 2 GB C: partition, Windows NT 4.0 Workstation, Service Pack 3, NTFS; 4 GB D: partition, Windows 2000 Professional, NTFS; 5 GB E: partition, data only, NTFS version 5.0. The system currently includes the built-in groups plus Personnel, Fiscal, and Manager groups. The E: drive includes a parent folder called Administration, for which Administrators have Full Control permission and Managers have Modify Control permission.

1. **Sheila, one of the managers, is in both the Administrator group and the Managers group. What are her permissions on this folder?**
   a. Full Control
   b. Modify
   c. Change
   d. No Access
2. **Sheila logs on and can manage the folder from the Windows 2000 Professional machine but cannot access the folder when she is logged on from the Windows NT 4.0 Workstation machine. What must she do to allow herself access from either operating system?**
   a. She must create duplicate groups in each operating system, and place each group in the permission's list.
   b. She must install Service Pack 4 or higher on the Windows NT 4.0 Workstation operating system.
   c. She will not be able to access these files from the Windows NT 4.0 Workstation machine.
   d. She must uncompress the folder.
3. **After Sheila gains access to the Administration folder, she creates two subfolders, Personnel and Fiscal. She wants all of the current permissions to remain in place and seeks to add the respective groups to each folder. How can she configure the folders in this way? (Choose all that apply.)**
   a. She must deselect the "Allow inheritable permissions" check box.
   b. She must select Copy when prompted.
   c. She must add each group to the respective folders.
   d. She must assign permissions to the new groups.
4. **The Administration folder is compressed. Sheila copies a file from the C: partition to this folder. Is the file compressed or uncompressed in its new location?**
   a. Compressed
   b. Uncompressed
5. **You discover that you are running low on drive space in your current partition and realize you have 4 GB of unused space. You format this new partition using FAT32. You assign F as the drive letter. Next, you decide to move the Fiscal folder to this new partition. Which group has access to the files? (Choose all that apply.)**
   a. Everyone
   b. Managers
   c. Fiscal
   d. Personnel

OBJECTIVES

2.18 Manage local security on files and folders

MANAGE LOCAL SECURITY • NTFS PERMISSIONS

UNDERSTANDING THE OBJECTIVE

After assigning proper NTFS permissions, you must manage these permissions. One of the simplest ways to do so is to assign permissions to groups rather than to individuals; this approach enables you to manage an individual's permissions based on the (most permissive) groups to which that user belongs. It's important to understand how moving and copying files between compressed and uncompressed folders and between partitions affects both their NTFS permissions and their compression states.

WHAT YOU REALLY NEED TO KNOW

- Access should be restricted as tightly as possible, while providing users the ability to do their jobs.
- Inheritance defaults and behaviors have changed in Windows 2000, as compared to Windows NT 4.0 permissions.
- Moving files and folders within a single partition retains the original permissions and compression settings.
- Moving files and folders between partitions causes the destination folder to inherit the original permissions and compression settings.
- Copying causes the destination folder (or file) to inherit the original permissions and compression settings, regardless of whether the target resides in the same partition as the original, or in a different partition.
- Moving or copying to FAT or FAT32 partitions removes all NTFS permissions from the target files.
- Anyone with Full Control can control the permissions on a folder.
- NTFS permissions are cumulative, so that they add across account settings and group memberships.

OBJECTIVES ON THE JOB

Usually, NTFS permissions are not the only permissions on a server; they are normally combined with Share permissions. For only NTFS permissions to apply, users must obtain physical access to the server and possess the "logon locally" user right (this is true by default only for Administrators and various classes of operators). When possible, change the Everyone group's Full Control default setting to something more restrictive. Do not use Deny unless a specific reason to do so exists. Control access through group memberships or implied denials through omission of certain groups. Recognize how moving and copying files affects NTFS and compression settings. Try some simple experiments to cement your understanding.

PRACTICE TEST QUESTIONS

1. **Printers may have both Share permissions and NTFS permissions.**
    a. True
    b. False
2. **What are the default permissions assigned to child objects (files and folders)?**
    a. Everyone—Full Control
    b. No permissions
    c. Permissions on the root of the partition
    d. Permissions inherited from the parent
3. **On a Windows 2000 member server, which groups can access the Admin$ share?**
    a. Administrators
    b. Backup Operators
    c. Everyone
    d. Power Users
4. **You have a database that is critical to your online courses. It maintains all exam scores, account logons, account information, user identification, and so on. The manager of the online courses quits suddenly, and you are worried that he might delete this database and other important files. How can you prevent him from accessing these files and ensure that his departure has minimal effects on other users? (Choose all that apply.)**
    a. Add his user account to the folder and select Deny—Full Control
    b. Select Deny—Full Control to any group of which he is a member that has access to the files and folders
    c. Lock his user account
    d. Add the Everyone group to the permissions list and set Deny—Full Control permission
5. **John has Modify permission on the Salary folder and Read & Execute and Write permissions on the Office folder. You move the entire Salary folder into the Office folder. What are John's permissions on the Salary folder now?**
    a. Full Control
    b. Modify
    c. Read & Execute and Write
    d. No Access
6. **Mary has Full Control permission on the Favorites folder in her user profile. She moves it to the network drive where her department's folder is located. She now belongs to two groups with the following permissions on the folder: Supervisors—Modify Marketing—Read and Write. What are Mary's permissions on the folder?**
    a. No Access
    b. Full Control
    c. Modify
    d. Read and Write

OBJECTIVES

2.19 Troubleshoot local security on files and folders

LOCAL SECURITY • NTFS PERMISSIONS • TROUBLESHOOTING

UNDERSTANDING THE OBJECTIVE

You should understand when new permissions take effect. The best way to deal with a single user's permissions is to break the connection to a server and let him or her create a new connection. You should understand what the Modify permission entails and be able to explain the effect of moving and copying files within and between partitions. FAT and FAT32 do not have local permissions. Instead, child objects inherit their permissions for parent objects. This concept is new to Windows 2000 and differs from the approach taken in Windows NT 4.0.

WHAT YOU REALLY NEED TO KNOW

- Always make sure that there are no denied access permissions when a user complains about not being able to access files or folders.
- When you add or correct user permissions, the affected user must log off or make a new connection to the computer before the new permissions will take effect.
- If you want users to be able to create, modify, and read files but not delete them, assign Read and Write permissions, but not Modify.
- If permissions are correct but a user has moved or copied files, you probably have to reset the permissions. Files typically inherit these settings from the destination folder unless they are moved within the same partition.
- Use the implied deny access by removing any group that you do not want to have access to resources. Only groups and users with defined permissions will then have access to the data.
- To see which users have files open, use the Computer Management snap-in.
- Place all home folders on an NTFS partition, separate from the operating system and applications.

OBJECTIVES ON THE JOB

Remove the Everyone group when possible, and assign the most restrictive permissions. In Windows 2000, the Modify permission has replaced the Change permission found in Windows NT 4.0. Inheritance now extends to child objects. To change permissions, you must clear the check box for allowing inherited permissions. Remember that the destination folder inherits permissions and compression settings unless it is moved within partitions. Ownership cannot be given; it must be taken. Most of the time, it is better not to assign permissions rather than to deny access.

PRACTICE TEST QUESTIONS

1. **You are trying to identify who currently has access to files on an NTFS partition. Which utility can you use to see which users are accessing files?**
   a. Shared Folder utility
   b. Disk Management utility
   c. Active Directory Users and Computers
   d. Event Viewer, System Log
2. **You cannot access the C$ share. Why not?**
   a. Only Administrators have access.
   b. Only Enterprise Administrators have access.
   c. Only Administrators and Server Operators have access.
   d. Only Administrators and Backup Operators have access.
3. **You have Full Control permission on a folder and want to prevent the Everyone group from accessing the D: drive, which contains all of your users' home directories. Your attempt fails. Why?**
   a. You are not an administrator.
   b. The check box for "Allow inherited permissions" is not selected.
   c. The check box for "Allow inherited permissions" is selected.
   d. The folder needs to be shared first.
4. **A new CFO comes on board at a famous Internet start-up company. He wants to take ownership of the previous CFO's files. What steps must he take? (Choose all that apply.)**
   a. As the Administrator, give him the Take Ownership permission.
   b. As the Administrator, assign him ownership of the files.
   c. As the Administrator, give him Modify permission.
   d. The CFO must take ownership.
5. **Which groups or users can assign permissions to files and folders? (Choose all that apply.)**
   a. Administrators
   b. Backup Operators
   c. Owner
   d. Server Operator
6. **You copy a read-only file, which you own, to a floppy. What will occur to the file when it is copied? (Choose all that apply.)**
   a. It will no longer be read-only.
   b. It will remain read-only.
   c. The file-level permissions will be removed.
   d. The file-level permissions will remain as they were.

OBJECTIVES

2.20 Configure access to files and folders via Web services

WEB SERVICES • ACCESS

UNDERSTANDING THE OBJECTIVE

You must understand how to enable and disable directory browsing, as well as how to use the **FTP** and FTP restart capabilities. You should also recognize how the Web access and NTFS permissions are combined when you are accessing Web resources. FrontPage extensions allow you to remotely manage file and folder structures and contents. You may configure this access by IP address and domain names.

WHAT YOU REALLY NEED TO KNOW

- Directory browsing may be set at the server, site, or directory level.
- Directory browsing settings may be forced to propagate to levels under which you are defining the setting.
- The FTP service in IIS allows for an FTP restart when downloading files with a client that also supports this service.
- FTP restart works only for files smaller than 4 GB that are downloaded to a client.
- FrontPage server extensions allow you to access your files remotely using FrontPage.
- You set access to pages through the server, site, or directory properties and NTFS properties.
- Use IP address and domain name restrictions in addition to Allow or Deny access permissions to files and folders.
- You must decide whether to allow anonymous FTP and Web access. Use the IUSR_<computername> account for this purpose.
- Use write, execute, and directory browsing options carefully, as their application opens up potential security problems.

OBJECTIVES ON THE JOB

Configuring access via Web services is an important job. Security should be the utmost concern when granting this type of access. Your goal should be to give users only the access they need—and absolutely no more. Be cautious when assigning write, execute, and browsing permissions. Execute permissions may allow dangerous scripts to run on your server that could compromise the network. Allowing directory browsing gives users some insight into your infrastructure.

PRACTICE TEST QUESTIONS

1. **All of your virtual directories have directory browsing allowed. The same is true for every new directory. How can you most efficiently disable this feature?**
   a. Clear directory browsing on the Web site
   b. Clear directory browsing on the Administrative site
   c. Shift-click to select all directories, click the properties, and clear directory browsing
   d. Clear directory browsing on the Web server
2. **You are aware that IIS 5.0 supports FTP restarts. You begin uploading a 250 MB file to the server but then lose your connection to your ISP. When you reconnect, the transfer does not restart. Why won't the system restart the uploading process?**
   a. Your FTP client does not support FTP restarts.
   b. You do not have permission to restart an FTP session.
   c. FTP restarts apply only to downloading.
   d. The file is too large for restarts.
3. **You want to run ASP scripts on your site. Which Web setting must you allow? (Choose all that apply.)**
   a. Read
   b. Write
   c. Modify
   d. Execute permissions, Scripts only
4. **To prevent .exe files from being downloaded, which of the following should you select? (Choose all that apply.)**
   a. Read access
   b. Write access
   c. Execute permissions, Scripts
   d. Execute permissions, Scripts and Executables
5. **To modify an .exe file, which of the following permissions must you have?**
   a. Read access
   b. Write access
   c. Execute permissions, Scripts
   d. Execute permissions, Scripts and Executables
6. **You want to run ASP scripts on your site. Which NTFS permission must you allow?**
   a. Read
   b. Write
   c. Modify
   d. Read & Execute

OBJECTIVES

2.21 Control access to files and folders via Web services

WEB SERVICES • ACCESS

UNDERSTANDING THE OBJECTIVE

The Administrative Web site enables you to configure access for users. You can create virtual directories to make file and folder access easier for remote users. You should understand how Dfs and redirects allow access to files as well as how to use content expiration controls file access.

WHAT YOU REALLY NEED TO KNOW

- HTML Internet Services Manager is no longer available through Administrative Tools.
- To access the Web version of the Internet Services Manager, find the **TCP** port being used by viewing the properties sheet for the Administrative Web site. Next, enter the server name followed by "*:portnumber*"—for example, http://Singapore:2788.
- Virtual directories may be local folders, Dfs folders, or folders on other machines.
- Virtual directories that are Dfs folders or reside on remote machines must be provided with a user name and password for access purposes when these directories are set up.
- When you are developing a remote site, the entire site or parts of the site may move. To make this operation transparent to users, you can open the properties sheet and redirect the site or folder to the new **URL**.
- Enable Content Expiration to make pages expire at specified times.

OBJECTIVES ON THE JOB

Use the **HTML** version of the Internet Services Manager to administer sites remotely. Virtual directories make it easier for remote users to access resources. You may use local folders, Dfs folders, or remote machines, even Windows 2000 Professional machines, for this purpose. URL redirection is helpful when you are making significant location changes on your site. Limit access to your site with content ratings, and enable Content Expiration so that your users can get current files.

PRACTICE TEST QUESTIONS

1. **What is the URL to access the HTML Internet Services Manager on a server called Webserver?**
    a. *webserver/administrative*
    b. *webserver:80/*
    c. *webserver:80/admin.asp*
    d. *webserver:<port#>*
2. **Your Web permissions are set to be more restrictive than both the Share permissions and the NTFS permissions. Which permissions are applied?**
    a. Web permissions
    b. Share permissions
    c. NTFS permissions
    d. Cumulative permissions
3. **Which user should be given Read access on the Web site to allow anonymous access?**
    a. Everyone
    b. Authenticated Users
    c. IUSR_Anonymous
    d. IUSR_*<computername>*
4. **You can specify access to only specific domains.**
    a. True
    b. False
5. **You can specify access to a specific IP address and a range of addresses.**
    a. True
    b. False
6. **Virtual directories can be ______________________. (Choose all that apply.)**
    a. local folders
    b. remote FAT32 folders
    c. Dfs folders
    d. NTFS files
7. **Which NTFS permission must be set to allow directory browsing from a browser?**
    a. Read
    b. List Folder Contents
    c. Write
    d. Modify

OBJECTIVES

2.22 Manage access to files and folders via Web services

MANAGE • WEB SERVICES • ACCESS

UNDERSTANDING THE OBJECTIVE

You should be able to manage access from the Administrative Web site as well as the local Internet Services Manager on the server. In addition, you should understand when and how to redirect access to files, and when and how to allow users to browse a directory if needed. You should also understand how to manage access through Web access permissions, NTFS permissions, IP addresses, and domain names.

WHAT YOU REALLY NEED TO KNOW

- You must be able to use the two methods that allow you to manage Web services.
- You can redirect Web changes to a new URL.
- You must be able to manage the ability to browse directories.
- Managing permissions relates to both Web permissions and NTFS permissions.
- You can also manage access via IP addresses and domain names.
- It is important to propagate changes throughout a site in an efficient and logical way.
- To manage the number of connections to resources, use the Connections option on the properties of the site or on the entire server.
- You can view current FTP sessions through the FTP Properties sheet.
- Web sites have unlimited connections by default; FTP sites support 100,000 connections by default.

OBJECTIVES ON THE JOB

To access the Internet Services Manager, you can use Administrative Tools on the server or work with a browser via the port number defined in the Administrative Web site. When you change a folder's location, consider using a redirect so that those files can continue to be found. You should enable directory browsing only if necessary, as doing so can provide information about your site's directory structure. The most restrictive permissions between Web and NTFS are applied when accessing Web resources. You may make changes to a server, a site, or a directory and then propagate those changes to the child nodes. You should limit the number of connections through the properties sheets of sites and servers, but you cannot set limitations to directories. View FTP sessions from the FTP Properties sheet; this ability is not available via the Web site or the server's properties sheets.

PRACTICE TEST QUESTIONS

1. **You must create the user IUSR *<computername>* before using this account as your anonymous logon account.**
    a. True
    b. False
2. **What is the default number of connections allowed to resources on a Web site?**
    a. 100
    b. 1000
    c. 10,000
    d. Unlimited
3. **Custom errors exist by default. Can can alter the text that is displayed with these messages?**
    a. Yes
    b. No
4. **A redirected URL may point to a(n) ________________. (Choose all that apply.)**
    a. exact URL
    b. directory below the URL
    c. permanent redirection for this resource
    d. several URLs
5. **After an upgrade to IIS 5.0, the location of the custom error messages changes.**
    a. True
    b. False
6. **You want to restrict access to folders by extending NTFS permissions to only users in your organization. Which of the following groups or users should not be in these folders?**
    a. Domain Users
    b. Domain Admins
    c. Everyone
    d. IUSR_*<computername>*
7. **You want to restrict access based on IP addresses. Which option is available to you? (Choose all that apply.)**
    a. Allow a single IP address.
    b. Allow an entire subnet.
    c. Deny access to a single IP address.
    d. Deny access to an entire subnet.

OBJECTIVES

2.23 Troubleshoot access to files and folders via Web services

TROUBLESHOOT • WEB SERVICES

UNDERSTANDING THE OBJECTIVE

You should know how to enable logging and understand what logging does. You should also understand where to view active users and open files. The Event Viewer may provide clues to some problems. You should know how access permissions work and what types of access are required by specific files. In addition, understand any error messages that appear.

WHAT YOU REALLY NEED TO KNOW

- You can enable logging from the server, the Web site, or a directory. The directory has a check box for "Log Visits," whereas servers and Web sites use the Enable logging option.
- You can detect access, both allowed and unauthorized, in the IIS log files, system log files, and security log files, depending on your configuration.
- To view open files, use the Shared utility in the Computer Management snap-in.
- You can view current FTP sessions from the FTP Properties sheet.
- In general, give the user IUSR_<computername> Read access to the wwwroot or default home directory when providing anonymous access.
- If **ASP** files won't run, check the Web permissions for Read Access and Scripts only Executable permissions.
- The default documents that a browser attempts to locate upon installation in the inetpub/wwwroot are default.htm, default.asp, and iishelp.asp. You can add files to this list or change the order in which these documents are parsed.

OBJECTIVES ON THE JOB

You should use and test IIS 5.0 extensively before you deploy it. Set the most restrictive permissions possible, and know how to view files that are being accessed. You should be able to configure your system to monitor access to files—usually unauthorized access only, unless a special reason exists to check successful connections. The IUSR_*<computername>* user should be given read-only NTFS access and the minimum permissions needed through the Web permissions. Remove Full Control permission for the Everyone group, and do not use the Deny access option. If you need to restart IIS, use the Restart IIS option with the IIS snap-in instead of restarting the server.

PRACTICE TEST QUESTIONS

1. **You attempt to connect from home to the company's intranet site but receive a "403.6 – Forbidden: IP address rejected" message. How can you correct this problem?**
   a. Obtain an IP address from the range of allowed IP addresses.
   b. Change the domain name on your home machine.
   c. Change the computer name on your home machine.
   d. Change the subnet mask on your home computer.
2. **In which folder are custom error messages stored?**
   a. \wwwroot\iishelp\common
   b. \wwwroot\help\common
   c. winnt\help\common
   d. winnt\help\iishelp\common
3. **Users who accessed your Web site earlier tell you they received a message stating "No Web site is configured at this address." What should you do first?**
   a. Make sure that the Web site or server's service is not stopped.
   b. Make sure that the default home directory is configured properly.
   c. Make sure that the default document has not been deleted.
   d. Make sure that the number of connections is not set too low.
4. **You can view current sessions for a Web site.**
   a. True
   b. False
5. **Which type of logging is available on IIS 5.0? (Choose all that apply.)**
   a. Windows 2000 Logging
   b. NCSA Common
   c. ODBC Logging
   d. W3C Extended
6. **You believe that someone is trying to illegally gain access to your FTP site. Where should you look for evidence that someone has attempted to log in if your server and Web site have been set up with the Microsoft defaults?**
   a. Application Event Log
   b. FTP Current Sessions
   c. Security Event Log
   d. System Event Log
7. **IIS log files can be used to detect unauthorized attempts to access your site.**
   a. True
   b. False

OBJECTIVES

2.24 Configure access to Web sites

CONFIGURE • WEB SITES

UNDERSTANDING THE OBJECTIVE

It is essential that you understand how to start and stop **WWW** and FTP services. You should be able to configure bandwidth throttling, process throttling, and application protection. Know which services are installed by default. You can deny or allow access based on either IP addresses or domain names. You should understand how to delegate control to different Web sites on a Web server and recognize the primary default ports associated with IIS.

WHAT YOU REALLY NEED TO KNOW

- You can stop both the FTP and WWW services via command-line utilities and the graphical interface.
- Instead of restarting the server, you may restart IIS only.
- You cannot restart IIS by using the browser version of Internet Services Manager.
- To manage your available bandwidth, use the Bandwidth Throttling option. This management can be performed at either the site or server level.
- You may specify how much of your processor to allocate to a site or server.
- Applications may be separated from the IIS process to protect them from bringing down IIS.
- Administrators or **ISP** owners can delegate a limited amount of administrative privileges to Web site owners. This setup allows some degree of flexibility without affecting other sites.
- Use the IUR_*<computername>* account on NTFS partitions with Read access when allowing anonymous access.
- Default primary ports include 21 (FTP), 23 (Telnet), 25 (**SMTP**), and 80 (**HTTP**).

OBJECTIVES ON THE JOB

The default settings for Bandwidth Throttling, Process Throttling, and Number of Connections are unlimited. Instead of rebooting your server, you may restart only IIS if desired. The Internet Services Manager (HTML) in version 4.0 remains available, but only through the browser. You must know the port number to connect via a browser; it is found in the properties sheet of the Administrative Web site. With multiple sites, you should grant Operators permission to each site to ease the administrative burden. You may also protect IIS and applications from one another through application pooling. If necessary, consider using some of the options for controlling the amount of processor usage or bandwidth through the throttling mechanisms. Deny access to domains and IP addresses when pertinent.

PRACTICE TEST QUESTIONS

1. **You are upgrading from Windows NT 4.0 running IIS 4.0 and want to preserve the IIS 4.0 installation. Is this possible?**
    a. Yes
    b. No
2. **What directory, installed by default, contains the wwwroot and ftproot subdirectories?**
    a. WINNT
    b. WINNT/Inetpub
    c. Inetpub
    d. IIS
3. **What is the default port number for the browser-based Internet Services Manager site?**
    a. 21
    b. 80
    c. 8080
    d. No default
4. **Members of the Operators group of any Web site may manage any Web site on the server.**
    a. True
    b. False
5. **What is the amount of bandwidth available to each site by default?**
    a. 10%
    b. 10 Kbps
    c. 10 Mbps
    d. No limit
6. **Your DHCP server's scope is set to give out addresses in the range of 194.151.71.10 through 194.151.71.254. Servers and routers use the static addresses of 194.151.71.1 through 194.151.71.9. You want to allow only computers on your subnet to access your site. How can you do this?**
    a. Set permission to Deny Access, except for the group of computers in the range 194.151.0.0 with a subnet mask of 255.255.0.0.
    b. Set permission to Deny Access, except for the group of computers in the range 194.151.71.0 with a subnet mask of 255.255.255.0.
    c. Set permission to Grant Access, except for the group of computers in the range 194.151.0.0 with a subnet mask of 255.255.0.0.
    d. Set permission to Grant Access, except for the group of computers in the range 194.151.71.0 with a subnet mask of 255.255.255.0.

OBJECTIVES

2.25 Manage access to Web sites

WEB SITES • MANAGE ACCESS

UNDERSTANDING THE OBJECTIVE

With the advent of Windows 2000, Integrated Windows Authentication is available for users with accounts in a Windows 2000 domain. Access permissions have also been changed slightly on the Document tab. Web permissions now apply to all browser users. If you use NTFS permissions, you will have more granular control for managing access to files and folders.

WHAT YOU REALLY NEED TO KNOW

- For ASP files to run on your Web site, you must have Read Web permissions and at least scripts defined in the executable permissions.
- To allow anonymous access, use the anonymous Web account, IUSR_<*computername*>, and assign Read NTFS permissions.
- The default location for your Web site is Inetpub/wwwroot.
- Basic authentication sends passwords in clear text; all other methods use some level of encryption.
- If you don't use one of the three default documents in each folder and at the root of your site, you should add this starting page to the list of documents in the Document tab.
- If your Web site's main page changes daily, consider setting Content Expiration to force reloads on your site on a daily basis.
- Web site Operators cannot create virtual directories on their sites.
- **NNTP** is the Network News Transfer Protocol, which is used for newsgroup services.
- NNTP is not installed by default.

OBJECTIVES ON THE JOB

When configuring and managing access to your site, you must consider whether anonymous access will be allowed to your Web and FTP site and decide how passwords will be transmitted across the Internet or LAN. In addition to determining who will be allowed access, you must manage Web permissions; with NTFS partitions, file and folder security becomes an issue. Default documents should be defined in the proper order. Grant the Operator permission to the appropriate, responsible people to assist in managing the site.

PRACTICE TEST QUESTIONS

Your company has a Web site. You are not concerned about who accesses the site—you want to allow anonymous access and don't care if passwords are sent in clear text. Your site's starting page is default.asp. On the properties sheet's Document tab, you select only the Script Source Access and Read check boxes.

1. **You selected the Integrated Windows Authentication option and checked the box for anonymous access. Will this choice satisfy the conditions you set forth concerning access permissions and the sending of clear-text passwords?**
   a. Yes
   b. No
2. **Users find that they cannot access your home page, even when they have valid Windows 2000 accounts. What should you change to allow users to access your site?**
   a. Uncheck Script Source Access.
   b. Select the check box for Write.
   c. Select the check box that states Allow ASP files to execute.
   d. Select Scripts Only from the Execute Permissions option.
3. **You have fine-tuned your site, and it now seems to be working well. During the day, you notice that users on your network have deleted some files. What is the most likely reason that users were allowed to delete the files?**
   a. The Anonymous user account has the Full Control permission.
   b. The special right, Delete, was granted to the domain users.
   c. Authenticated users have Modify permissions.
   d. The Everyone group has Full Control.
4. **You want to create a virtual directory that is accessible only from computers on your subnet and then list the contents of that directory. Which option can you accomplish for this virtual directory only?**
   a. Limiting access to your subnet
   b. Listing the contents of the directory
   c. None of the above
   d. Both a and b
5. **Which command must you type on the command line to start the IIS service?**
   a. net start wwwsrv
   b. net start w3srv
   c. net start w3svc
   d. net start iissrv

OBJECTIVES

2.26 Control access to Web sites

WEB SITES • CONTROL ACCESS

UNDERSTANDING THE OBJECTIVE

Controlling access to Web sites with IIS 5 and Windows 2000 is similar to the situation with Windows NT in many ways. You can control access with NTFS permissions if files are on NTFS partitions, restrict access based on IP addresses and domain names, control the type of access to files, and delegate control to each Web site.

WHAT YOU REALLY NEED TO KNOW

- IIS can host multiple hosts in three ways in Windows 2000: by using separate IP addresses, by using different host headers, or by changing the port numbers.
- The TCP port assigned to the administrative site is between 2000 and 9999.
- Digest Authentication is a new Windows 2000 protocol used to access a site. It is supported only in Windows 2000 domains, and only the latest browsers support this protocol.
- Integrated Windows Authentication is used only when the Anonymous account does not have access to the site. Kerberos security is also available with this protocol when you are using IE 5.x.
- Web permissions apply to any user accessing a Web site.
- Two security templates are available to assist you in configuring your Web site—the Public Web Site template and the Secure Web Site template. The Secure template is intended for domain members.
- Members of the Operators group can set the following items: Web Site access permissions, logging, default documents, content expiration, and ratings.
- You should use Execute permissions. Use Scripts only—not Script source access—to allow ASP files to run.
- Use Custom Error messages to display information that users should see on your own custom background.

OBJECTIVES ON THE JOB

You have many options for controlling access to your site. You may also grant or deny access via IP addresses or domain names. Additionally, the type of access that all Web users have is defined in the Home Directory tab.

PRACTICE TEST QUESTIONS

You have set up a Web site, *www.mycompany.com*, that uses the defaults assigned at the time of installation. You know how to create a reasonably secure intranet site. You now create a new site called *intranet.mycompany.com* and change some of the settings. The home directory is now on an NTFS partition in the Inetpub/Intranet directory with the default NTFS settings. You change the port to 9800. You set the Web permissions to Read, with Execute Permissions set at None. You add the Webmasters group to the Operators group for this site.

1. **You tell users that they may access the intranet site by visiting *intranet.mycompany.com*, but the users complain that they cannot access the site. Which URL should users employ to access the site?**
   a. *intranet.mycompany.com*
   b. *intranet.mycompany.com/9800*
   c. *intranet.mycompany.com:9800*
   d. *www.intranet.mycompany.com*
2. **You discover that anonymous users have access to your Web site and want to eliminate this access through the use of NTFS permissions. How do you do so? (Choose all that apply.)**
   a. Remove the Everyone group.
   b. Deny Full Control to the Everyone group.
   c. Add the Domain Users group with at least Read control.
   d. Remove the IUSR_<*computername*> account.
3. **Your Web developer creates the main page for the intranet and calls it index.html. When they visit this site, however, users cannot access this file. Give two ways to solve this problem.**
   a. Use *http://www.intranet.mycompany.index.html.*
   b. Use *http://intranet.mycompany.com:8080.html.*
   c. Add the default document, index.html, and move to the top of the list.
   d. Remove the default.htm and default.asp files from the default document list.
4. **Your Web developer, who is a member of the Webmasters group, wants to create a new virtual directory. How should the Web developer accomplish this task?**
   a. The developer should access the intranet site via a browser and create the directory.
   b. The developer should access the intranet site via a server and create the directory.
   c. The Administrator should access the intranet site from the server and create the directory.
   d. The Administrator should access the intranet site from the browser and create the directory.

OBJECTIVES

2.27 Troubleshoot access to Web sites

IIS • FTP • PING

UNDERSTANDING THE OBJECTIVE

Troubleshooting web access has been improved in Windows 2000. Applications can be set to run isolated from the IIS services, preventing a failed application from crashing a server. Performance tuning is still available, as well as bandwidth and process throttling to allocate resources to different sites. Three items, which can differentiate sites in IIS 5.0 are the port number, the host header, and the IP address. Any one change may differentiate your sites. Host headers are not supported in some older browsers.

WHAT YOU REALLY NEED TO KNOW

- Exceeding the tuning defined on the Performance page hurts the memory allocation for that site.
- The default port number for public Web sites is 80.
- The event log may be used to view unauthorized attempts to log onto your FTP site and any secured sites.
- Operators may not create virtual directories.
- FrontPage extensions are enabled by default, as is logging.
- The Browser Capabilities Component may be used to determine a browser's capability and update the browscap.ini file as new browsers are released.
- Indexing is enabled by default.

OBJECTIVES ON THE JOB

Troubleshooting your Web server is relatively easy after it has been configured. Many times, starting and stopping the service solves the problem. Always ensure that you have TCP/IP connectivity when users tell you they cannot access your site. The easiest way to do this is to PING the Ip address or name of the computer. If you must restart IIS, use the IIS Restart instead of rebooting the machine. View current FTP sessions via the FTP Properties sheet.

PRACTICE TEST QUESTIONS

Your Windows 2000 member server is running IIS 5.0 and hosts five Web sites, each with its own unique name. You tuned each site based on performance levels defined in the service agreements with each site owner. All agreements require you to provide usage statistics to each site owner on a weekly basis. Additionally, each site owner is allowed one person to act as the site administrator. Some of the sites may include custom applications to run their banner ads and Web stores. All sites must support Frontpage extensions.

1. **One of the sites suddenly has a surge in hits and exceeds the tuning you set of 100,000 hits per day. Which component is most affected by this surge?**
   a. Hard drive access
   b. Memory
   c. Processor
   d. Bandwidth
2. **A site that includes a banner ad application occasionally causes IIS to crash. What is the best use of resources while protecting the other four sites from being affected?**
   a. Protect each Web site through the Application Protection option.
   b. Isolate the banner ad application from the IIS services.
   c. Place this Web site with the banner add application on a separate server.
   d. Convert the standalone server to a domain controller.
3. **When attempting to access a Web site, you receive the message, "The page cannot be found." What causes this?**
   a. The Anonymous account has not been set up.
   b. The Web site is on a FAT partition.
   c. The default port number has changed.
   d. The home directory points to the ftproot directory instead of wwwroot.
4. **When you prepare to send the weekly usage report, you find there is no data to send. What should you check first?**
   a. Was the log file deleted?
   b. Was logging enabled?
   c. Was the log file initially set up on an NTFS partition?
   d. Is there sufficient disk space to allow logging?
5. **A user running IE 2.x cannot access a site but can access the default Web site. What is most likely to cause this error?**
   a. Host headers are not supported in that version of Internet Explorer.
   b. TCP/IP is not installed on the client.
   c. TCP/IP is not bound to the Web site the user is accessing.
   d. IE 2.x does not support non-standard port numbers.

Section 3

Configuring and Troubleshooting Hardware Devices and Drivers

OBJECTIVES

3.1 Configure hardware devices

DEVICE MANAGER • IRQ SHARING AND STEERING • RESOURCES • ACPI

UNDERSTANDING THE OBJECTIVE

After installing a Windows 2000 operating system, you may need to either install new hardware devices or reconfigure the existing ones native to the system. Therefore, you must be completely familiar with this procedure and its many characteristics. Windows 2000 offers a plethora of configuration settings that you must know to achieve successful operation of the system as a whole.

WHAT YOU REALLY NEED TO KNOW

- Windows 2000 fully supports Plug and Play and is optimized for use with computers with **ACPI** system boards. Plug and Play supports many devices, including **PCI**, **ISA**, **SCSI**, and **USB**.
- The main port of call for hardware device configuration and information is Computer Management. Here, you can delve into the Device Manager and System Information snap-ins for the lowdown on your computer hardware.
- The Add/Remove Hardware, Display, Network and Dial-up Connections, Phone and Modem Options, and Power Options applets in the Control Panel can also be used for hardware device installation and configuration.
- There are two main ways to install a device. If the device is Plug and Play-compliant, turn the machine off, insert the device, and start Windows 2000. The device should be automatically detected and installed. If the device is not Plug and Play-compliant, the Add/Remove Hardware Wizard can be used to manually install the device.
- Windows 2000 supports **IRQ** sharing. If no IRQ is not available for a device, Windows 2000 assigns it the IRQ of 9, which by default is shared. Windows 2000 also supports PCI IRQ steering, which can dynamically reassign PCI device resource requirements if necessary.

OBJECTIVES ON THE JOB

This objective essentially centers on the overall configuration of hardware devices. For that reason, it is difficult to give specific advice related to it. You should thoroughly understand all of the applets and snap-ins mentioned herein and know how they can be used to configure a hardware device. You are strongly urged to carry out the installation and removal of as many hardware devices as is practicable on your Windows 2000 Server lab machine. This exercise will ensure that you appreciate the finite configuration settings that are available.

One item worth a further mention is the ability of Windows 2000 to share IRQs, which eliminates the device conflicts that caused many headaches under Windows NT 4.0. Although Windows 2000 normally sorts out device conflicts on its own, you may need to assign the IRQ reserved for sharing—the default is IRQ 9—to a PCI device to overcome any lingering conflicts.

PRACTICE TEST QUESTIONS

1. **What is required to take full advantage of the Plug and Play technology? (Choose all that apply.)**
   a. A Plug and Play operating system
   b. ACPI BIOS or Plug and Play BIOS
   c. Plug and Play-compliant hardware devices and drivers
   d. An IRQ sharing driver
2. **Although Plug and Play devices can be hot-plugged, some devices, such as modems, network cards, and removable storage devices, should not be disconnected while Windows 2000 is running.**
   a. True
   b. False
3. **Which of the following can be Plug and Play devices? (Choose all that apply.)**
   a. SCSI devices
   b. ISA devices
   c. PCI devices
   d. USB devices
4. **You have five Windows 2000 Server computers that need upgrading with various components. Identify the correct installation procedure for each of the following new components. (Choose all that apply.)**
   Server 1 Monitor
   Server 2 PCI Plug and Play modem
   Server 3 PCI Plug and Play 100 MB Ethernet adapter
   Server 4 Additional CPU
   Server 5 ISA non-Plug and Play modem

   a. Turn off the computer, install the device, and restart the computer.
   b. Turn off the computer, install the device, and restart the computer. Use the Add/Remove Hardware Wizard to install the device.
   c. Turn off the computer, install the device, and restart the computer. Use Device Manager to install the correct HAL for the system.
   d. Use the Display applet in the Control Panel to specify the correct driver.
5. **Where does Windows 2000 get the information required to build the PCI IRQ steering table that enables it to dynamically allocate resources to hardware devices?**
   a. From RAM
   b. From the CMOS chip on a particular device's hardware PCI card
   c. From the system BIOS
   d. The CPU performs the calculations necessary to build the PCI IRQ steering table.

OBJECTIVES

3.2 Configure driver signing options

DIGITAL SIGNATURE • SIGNATURE VERIFICATION AND CHECKING

UNDERSTANDING THE OBJECTIVE

A new feature of Windows 2000 is driver signing. It ensures that drivers meet certain stringent Microsoft standards and have not been tampered with since their origination; thus drivers will be less likely to cause problems with Windows 2000. Device drivers that pass a series of tests administered by the Windows Hardware Quality Lab are given a digital signature to verify their integrity.

WHAT YOU REALLY NEED TO KNOW

- A digital signature is a means for the creator of a file to verify that it belongs to that user and has not been altered in any way since its inception.
- Microsoft, digitally signed all device drivers found on the Windows 2000 CD-ROM, including those of third-party vendors, to signify its approval of their use with Windows 2000.
- Windows 2000 possesses the capability to warn a user that it is about to install unsigned driver code, in addition to preventing such installations.
- Included in Windows 2000 is the Signature Verification tool (SIGVERIF.EXE), which allows you to scan files (either the system as a whole or files found in a specified location) on a machine to determine whether they have been signed.
- A Windows 2000 Administrator can also implement Signature Checking by setting driver signing options in the System applet in the Control Panel.
- Driver signing also plays a part in unattended installations. It's possible to set the driver signing policy in the answer file of an unattended installation by using the DriverSigningPolicy key in the [Unattended] section. The parameters are Ignore, Warn, or Block (as above); the default is Warn.

OBJECTIVES ON THE JOB

A common misconception regarding Windows NT 4.0 is that it is an unstable operating system that needs rebooting at regular intervals due to inherent flaws. In fact, Windows NT 4.0 suffers from poorly written device drivers from third-party vendors that cause problems with the base operating system. Microsoft has attempted to remedy this situation with the introduction of driver signing to ensure that drivers meet a suitable standard and do not contain poorly written code. Microsoft strongly advises against implementing a policy whereby driver signing is ignored (for example, using the DriverSigningPolicy=Ignore key in an answer file), unless the device driver in question has been comprehensively tested in the environment in which it is to be implemented.

PRACTICE TEST QUESTIONS

1. **What is a digital signature, as referred to in the context of driver signing?**
    a. A coder's inscribed personal signature on a file
    b. The time and date and modified stamp on a file
    c. A means of verifying that a file has been unaltered and the originator can be confidently and positively identified
    d. A means of verifying that a file has been altered and the originator cannot be confidently and positively identified
2. **Susan, a network administrator, joined a new company that has both Windows 2000 Server computers and Professional clients. Some of the servers are exhibiting strange symptoms, and Susan suspects that they do not have digitally signed device drivers installed. How can she verify this fact in the most efficient way possible?**
    a. Run the SIGVERIF.EXE utility.
    b. Run the SIGCHECK.EXE utility.
    c. Run the DIGISIGCHECK.EXE utility.
    d. View the properties of each driver file to determine if it is digitally signed.
3. **Tom, the Windows 2000 network administrator for a prominent software company, needs to deploy 200 Windows 2000 Professional machines on the network. He wants to enforce a driver signing policy that prevents the installation of unsigned drivers on these machines. How can he implement this policy in an unattended setup?**
    a. In the [Driver Signing Policy] section of the answer file, include the line Prevent.
    b. In the [Unattended] section of the answer file, use the key: DriverSigningPolicy=Prevent.
    c. In the [Unattended] section of the answer file, use the key: DriverSigningPolicy=Block.
    d. On the Windows 2000 deployment computer, create a Group Policy that calls for rejecting unsigned device drivers.
4. **What are the correct meanings of the Signature Checking levels? (Choose all that apply.)**
    a. Level 0: equivalent to Ignore; installs all files irrespective of the presence of a file signature
    b. Level 1: equivalent to Warn; users are prompted with a warning dialog before the installation of unsigned drivers
    c. Level 2: equivalent to Block; users are prevented from installing files without a valid digital signature
    d. Level 1: equivalent to Ignore; installs all files irrespective of the presence of a file signature
    e. Level 2: equivalent to Warn; users are prompted with a warning dialog before the installation of unsigned drivers
    f. Level 3: equivalent to Block; users are prevented from installing files without a valid digital signature

OBJECTIVES

3.3 Update device drivers

WINDOWS UPDATE • UPDATE DRIVERS

UNDERSTANDING THE OBJECTIVE

Updating device drivers is a critical operation needed to keep your Windows 2000 systems running smoothly. Microsoft and other vendors frequently release updated drivers for products that need to be installed on the appropriate machines in any given network. This objective discusses ways to implement device driver upgrades.

WHAT YOU REALLY NEED TO KNOW

- In essence, there are two fundamental ways in which to update device drivers: through Windows Update or by using the Update Device Driver Wizard.
- If you are not going the **WU** route, then Device Manager is your destination to update device drivers. To initiate the **UDDW**, click the Update button on the Driver tab of a device's properties in **DM**.
- Note that administrative privileges are required to update device drivers by either of the above methods.
- The actual permissions required for a user to install device drivers are the Load\Unload Drivers privilege and Copy permission to the Registry.
- You can use the runas command to run utilities or programs that require privileges different than those possessed by the current user.
- Windows 2000 looks for drivers for a particular device in its driver database located in the driver cabinet file (DRIVER.CAB) first, even if another location has been specified when running the UDDW. By default, this file is located in the %systemroot% \Driver Cache\<platform>\ directory.
- Windows 2000 does not always associate the correct, or most recent, driver it finds from its driver database for a device.

OBJECTIVES ON THE JOB

It's imperative that the correct (Windows 2000 specific) drivers be used for a hardware device. Installing an incorrect driver can result in a device failing to function correctly, or at all. Using incorrect drivers for monitors can have costly and far-reaching ramifications. Severe damage can be inflicted on monitors by using incorrect drivers and display settings. Accordingly, you should ensure that you have the correct Windows 2000 driver for the monitor.

PRACTICE TEST QUESTIONS

1. **Where is the DRIVER.CAB file located by default?**
    a. %systemroot% \system32\drivers\
    b. %systemroot% \Driver Cache\I386\
    c. %systemroot% \Inf\
    d. %systemroot% \system32\Driver Cache\I386\
2. **Bill wants to update critical system files and drivers on a Windows 2000 member server. While working on the computer, he runs Windows Update, but receives an error message indicating that he has insufficient privileges to continue. To which group should Bill belong when logging on interactively to the member server?**
    a. The Domain Admin global group in the domain belonging to the member server
    b. The Administrators global group in the domain belonging to the member server
    c. The Administrators local group
    d. The Domain Administrators global group
3. **You want to update a driver for your monitor on a Windows 2000 Server computer. You select a driver from the Microsoft list, and a warning message appears. How should you proceed?**
    a. Run Windows Update to ensure that you have the latest drivers for the monitor.
    b. Obtain the latest driver for the monitor from the vendor and use it instead of the Microsoft-suggested driver.
    c. Obtain the latest driver for the monitor from Microsoft and use it instead of the Microsoft-suggested driver.
    d. Run the Update Device Driver Wizard and use the driver that is suggested, even if it is not an exact match for the vendor's monitor.
4. **Sue is asked to provide remote access for users of her company via a dial-up connection. She installs a modem in the appropriate Windows 2000 Server. Plug and Play detects the modem and installs a driver for it. Sue then installs and correctly configures Routing and Remote Access. She tests the setup from a user's remote machine, but is unable to establish a connection with the server. What could cause this problem? (Choose all that apply.)**
    a. The client machine is configured incorrectly.
    b. Routing and Remote Access is configured incorrectly for the modem.
    c. Plug and Play has installed an incorrect driver for the modem.
    d. Although the server has Routing and Remote Access installed, it is not enabled.

OBJECTIVES

3.4 Troubleshooting problems with hardware

TROUBLESHOOT • DIAGNOSE • REMEDY

UNDERSTANDING THE OBJECTIVE

Some people consider troubleshooting to be a "black art", and perhaps they're right. Nevertheless, Windows 2000 does a good job of lessening the everyday difficulties that an administrator can face in pursuit of a smooth-running network. In essence, troubleshooting focuses on knowledge and its application. Although one could write a sizable tome on the subject, we'll concentrate on categorical aspects in Windows 2000.

WHAT YOU REALLY NEED TO KNOW

- Device Manager and the Add/Remove Hardware Wizard in the Control Panel are the primary tools for resolving hardware problems.
- Device Manager allows you to access the particular properties for a hardware device and, in some cases, such as a modem, allows you to perform diagnostic functions. These activities are helpful in troubleshooting dilemmas.
- Although it is not obvious, the Add/Remove Hardware Wizard has a troubleshooting mode as well. The second screen of the wizard includes the option to Add/Troubleshoot a device.
- Windows 2000 comes with troubleshooters in the native Help files that can assist in resolving hardware device problems. Many troubleshooters exist, including Hardware and more specific Modem, Display, and Routing and Remote Access tools.
- A tricky issue under Windows 2000 is display adapters and monitors. If Windows 2000 installs the correct driver, all is well; in most cases, Windows 2000 will disallow any unsupported settings. If Windows "thinks" it has the correct drivers installed, however, then it may allow settings that are unsupported, which could result in damage to the monitor.
- You can also configure multiple hardware profiles for a machine. While this issue is more applicable to Windows 2000 Professional running on a laptop, for example, it's important to understand multiple hardware profiles' use and application.

OBJECTIVES ON THE JOB

Nothing beats outright knowledge when it comes to troubleshooting. For this reason, you are strongly encouraged to cultivate a comprehensive personal knowledge base of information relating to installing, uninstalling, and diagnosing hardware-based problems on Windows 2000 systems. Another critical point is having the latest drivers for a hardware device. Preferably, these drivers should be signed, for reasons discussed in earlier objectives in this section. Always use a newer vendor driver over an older Microsoft driver, as the former doubtless supersedes the latter and offers either better performance, increased reliability, or both.

PRACTICE TEST QUESTIONS

1. **Where can you start the Add/Remove Hardware Wizard? (Choose all that apply.)**
   a. The Add/Remove Hardware applet in the Control Panel
   b. The Hardware Wizard button on the Hardware tab of the System applet in the Control Panel
   c. From the Run dialog box
   d. From the command line

2. **How can you remove hardware devices from Windows 2000? (Choose all that apply.)**
   a. Use the Add/Remove Hardware Wizard.
   b. Uninstall a device from within Device Manager.
   c. Disable a device from within Device Manager.
   d. Uninstall a device from the Hardware applet in the Control Panel.

3. **Kevin, who is the network administrator for a small software company, attempts to remove a modem from a Windows 2000 Server that appears to have developed a fault. He runs the Add/Remove Hardware Wizard to remove the modem. The process hangs and continues to hang after Kevin makes repeated attempts to remove the modem. How can he proceed?**
   a. Use Device Manager to remove the faulty modem.
   b. Remove the modem and reboot the server.
   c. Disable the modem.
   d. Create a new hardware profile for the modem.

4. **You want to specify a higher resolution setting for your current monitor, but Windows 2000 displays a warning message and does not allow it. How can you achieve the higher resolution?**
   a. Download and use the latest driver for the monitor from Microsoft's Web site.
   b. Download and use the latest driver for the monitor from the vendor's Web site.
   c. Remove the existing monitor driver, scan the system for hardware changes, and select the correct driver from the list when prompted.
   d. Use the Force Driver setting in Device Manager to compel Windows 2000 to use the existing driver with the settings specified.

Section 4

Managing, Monitoring, and Optimizing System Performance, Reliability, and Availability

OBJECTIVES

4.1 Monitor usage of system resources

SYSTEM MONITOR • PERFORMANCE MONITOR • TASK MANAGER

UNDERSTANDING THE OBJECTIVE

In Windows 2000, many improvements have been made to the Windows NT 4.0 utilities, and several new utilities have been added to monitor your resources. Alerts have been improved in the Performance Monitor, quotas and encryption are available by default on NTFS partitions, you can assign processes to processors on multiple-processor machines, and a disk defragmentation tool is now native to Windows 2000.

WHAT YOU REALLY NEED TO KNOW

- Set warnings before quotas are reached to alert users that they are using too much disk space.
- Note that the Disk Defragmenter has two options: Analyze and Defrag. Analyze your system with Disk Defragmenter before defragging it, as this step may not be necessary.
- Use the Assign affinities option on multiple-processor machines to assign a process to a specific processor.
- Use the **SNMP** service to monitor devices that are capable of being SNMP agents.
- Set alternative colors in the Tools menu item for compressed folders, so as to easily identify compressed files and folders.
- Use the Task Manager to obtain a quick view of processes used, percentage of the processor used, and amount of memory allocated.
- Enable logical disk counters with the diskperf – yv command and enable all counters with the diskperf – y command. A restart is required after initiating this command.
- Using System Monitor, make sure that the following values are not exceeded: Disk Queue=2, % processor time <80%, available memory> 4 MB, and Pages/sec <20.
- Note that 16-bit programs are monitored via their **NTVDM** counters.

OBJECTIVES ON THE JOB

Windows 2000, offers many tools to monitor your network and servers. One of the easiest to use is the Task Manager. With this utility, you can view information about every process on the server, the amount of memory available, and so on. You can also use it to manage resources by ending processes, setting their priorities, or binding to a specific processor. The System Monitor can provide information about your hardware and software. The Network Monitor can give information about your network and is not installed by default. Quotas can assist in monitoring disk usage, and a quick glance of every user's usage can be obtained by clicking the Quota Entries button.

PRACTICE TEST QUESTIONS

You are configuring your first Windows 2000 member server. In doing so, you wish to make it very easy to monitor the disk usage by users as well as by groups. You want to warn users if they are using too much disk space and quickly determine whether a file or folder is compressed. You need to monitor logical and physical disk statistics and provide real-time monitoring of network packets. You format all volumes with NTFS and install all default options.

1. **Which of the following is not possible with the example installation? (Choose all that apply.)**
   a. Monitor disk usage by user.
   b. Monitor disk usage by group.
   c. Monitor logical disk by statistics.
   d. Monitor physical disk by statistics.
2. **Which of the following is possible after installing nondefault options? (Choose all that apply.)**
   a. Monitor disk usage by user.
   b. Monitor disk usage by group.
   c. Monitor network packets.
   d. Set performance alerts.
3. **You want to set disk quotas on all users and have selected the Enable Disk Quotas check box. How much space does each user have as the default quota?**
   a. 1 byte
   b. 1 KB
   c. 1 MB
   d. 10 MB
4. **In addition to implementing the diskperf –y command to enable all disk counters, what must be done before you can monitor these counters?**
   a. Install Network Monitor.
   b. Install Performance Monitor.
   c. Install SNMP service.
   d. Reboot the system.
5. **When you originally set up the machine, you wanted the ability to just glance at files and folders to see whether they are compressed. You have compressed some files, but it isn't obvious that they are actually compressed. What else should you do?**
   a. Enable alternative colors under the Advanced tab in the folder properties sheet.
   b. Enable alternative colors in the Tools menu for compressed folders.
   c. Select the check box for Enable Compression with Alternative Colors.
   d. Reboot the system.
6. **You wish to set 20 MB quotas on all users except network administrators or officers of the company. Can you do so?**
   a. Yes
   b. No

OBJECTIVES

4.2 Optimize usage of system resources

SYSTEM MONITOR • PERFORMANCE MONITOR • TASK MANAGER • OPTIMIZE • DISK CLEANUP • QUOTA MANAGER • DISK DEFRAGMENTER • SCANDISK

UNDERSTANDING THE OBJECTIVE

Windows 2000 includes new tools to assist Administrators in optimizing system resources. Among these new features are Disk Cleanup, Quota Manager, and Disk Defragmenter. Disk Cleanup can delete temporary files and temporary Internet files, compress seldom-used files, empty the Recycle Bin, and remove rarely or never used applications. Disk Defragmenter can place fragmented files in a contiguous space to optimize system performance. Quota Manager can prevent users from placing too much data on drives. Dynamic disks are now used in Windows 2000; when creating mirrors, striped volumes, and RAID volumes, they are no longer called "sets" as they were in Windows NT 4.0.

WHAT YOU REALLY NEED TO KNOW

- ◆ Use Quota Manager tool to first warn and then deny users the ability to save files to a drive. This tool automatically manages hard drive space for you.
- ◆ Defragment your system periodically after analysis determines that this step is necessary.
- ◆ Set the Affinity on processes to bind a process to a specific processor.
- ◆ Use Disk Cleanup to automate the removal of useless files.
- ◆ Use compression to save disk space.
- ◆ Copying files from one compressed folder to another creates a performance drag as the files are first uncompressed, then copied, and finally recompressed.
- ◆ You can find Disk Defragmenter in the Computer Management snap-in and on the Tools tab of the drive's properties sheet.
- ◆ Disk Defragmenter works on all file systems.
- ◆ Compression, quotas, and encryption work only on NTFS volumes.

OBJECTIVES ON THE JOB

Quota Manager and Disk Defragmenter are two utilities that were available for Windows NT 4.0 as third-party add-ons and that were requested by many Administrators. Enabling Quota Manager optimizes the use of disk space, whereas Disk Defragmenter optimizes access to files. Disk Cleanup eliminates the need for Administrators to look for temporary files all over a system so as to delete them. In addition, it highlights files and programs that are not used or used only rarely and gives you the option to compress or delete files.

PRACTICE TEST QUESTIONS

You installed Windows 2000 Advanced Server about 10 months ago. At the time, you formatted the C: and D: partitions with NTFS and the E: partition with FAT32. Drive O contains 5 MB of unallocated space. Drive 1 contains the 2 GB F: partition formatted with FAT16, and the remainder is unallocated space. All disks are 20 GB dynamic disks. The only third-party software installed is an antivirus program.

1. **Lately, users have been complaining that it is taking too long to access their files on the E: partition. What should you do first on the server?**
   a. Analyze the drive using Disk Defragmenter.
   b. Defragment the partition.
   c. Run ScanDisk.
   d. Install the latest service pack.
2. **The Disk Defragmenter utility can be used on which drives? (Choose all that apply.)**
   a. C:
   b. D:
   c. E:
   d. F:
3. **You sometimes delete unused files but then forget to empty the Recycle Bin. You want to automate both the deletion of temporary files and emptying of the Recycle Bin. Which utility accomplishes this task for all partitions?**
   a. Disk Cleanup
   b. Drive Cleanup
   c. Partition Cleanup
   d. No utility works for all of the partitions.
4. **You believe that some of your files may have errors. After running ScanDisk, you discover errors, but ScanDisk does not automatically fix them. What should you do to allow ScanDisk to automatically fix the errors? (Choose all that apply.)**
   a. Nothing, ScanDisk allows only manual fixes.
   b. Restart your computer in safe mode.
   c. Close all open files.
   d. Disable your antivirus software.
5. **You want to improve the read and write performance on your drives. How can you do so on the machine previously described?**
   a. Create a mirrored volume.
   b. Create a stripe set.
   c. Create a striped volume.
   d. Create a RAID 5 volume.

OBJECTIVES

4.3 Manage processes

MANAGE PROCESSES

UNDERSTANDING THE OBJECTIVE

In Windows 2000, you can manage processes with many tools: Performance Monitor, System Monitor, Task Manager, the Service applet, and command-line utilities. From within Performance Monitor, you can create charts, logs, and alerts. All 16-bit programs are always started in the same address space unless explicitly defined or started in their own separate space.

WHAT YOU REALLY NEED TO KNOW

- Within Performance Monitor, counter logs are used to monitor system performance over specified time intervals.
- Within Performance Monitor, trace logs are used to continuously monitor hardware and services.
- Within Performance Monitor, you can set alerts on processes that may be causing problems.
- Start programs in their own address space by entering stat /separate <*program*> on the command line or by selecting the appropriate check box on the properties of the shortcut thereby indicating that the program should start in its own address space.
- To monitor 16-bit programs with System Monitor, you need to view the % Processor in Process object. If separate NTVDMs exist, you must choose one or more of the instances.
- The Processes tab in the Task Manager includes default columns for Name, Process ID, CPU, CPU Time, and Memory Usage. You may add others using the Options menu.
- For services that are not needed, in the Services applet, either configure them to start manually or disable the services.

OBJECTIVES ON THE JOB

In Windows 2000, knowing which tool to use and when to use it can help Administrators fine-tune and troubleshoot their networks. Performance Monitor can be used to gather baseline data and send alerts. System Monitor can be used for real-time troubleshooting of hardware and software. Task Manager is a quick and efficient method for checking memory and processor usage, viewing information about a specific process, changing the priority of a process, or simply ending the process. Use the Services applet to have a service stop and start automatically or manually, or even to disable a service.

PRACTICE TEST QUESTIONS

You are running Windows 2000 Server on a dual-Pentium 400 machine. You must run two 16-bit programs—fiscal1.exe and fiscal2.exe—for your fiscal office. In addition, you must run several other programs, some of which do not have the highest priority in your organization. All disks are dynamic and formatted with NTFS.

1. **You want to start each 16-bit program in a separate address space. You do not want to do so from the command line every time you launch the applications. How do you accomplish this task?**
   a. Using the command line is the only way.
   b. Start each program using Task Manager, right-click each NTVDM instance, and select Run in new NTVDM.
   c. Select the properties of the shortcut to each application, and then select the Run in separate memory space check box.
   d. Select the properties of the shortcut to each application, and then select the Run in separate NTVDM check box.
2. **Your server has many processes that are currently running. You suspect that one process is consuming a disproportionate amount of your CPU's time. Which tool will allow you to quickly determine the CPU usage and investigate and stop the offending process?**
   a. Event Viewer
   b. Performance Monitor
   c. System Monitor
   d. Task Manager
3. **You want to utilize System Monitor to determine the effects of each program running on your system. Which counter should you monitor?**
   a. % Processor for the Process object
   b. % Processor for the Processor object
   c. % Processor for the Server object
   d. % Processor for the Thread object
4. **You can change the priorities of your less important programs using Task Manager.**
   a. True
   b. False
5. **In Task Manager, you notice that the lsass.exe process is using approximately 80% of your CPU's time. When you try to end the process, you cannot. Why not?**
   a. You are not an Enterprise Administrator.
   b. You are not a Domain Administrator.
   c. You are not a Server Operator.
   d. This essential service cannot be stopped in Task Manager.

OBJECTIVES

4.4 Set priorities on processes

PROCESSES • SETTING PRIORITIES

UNDERSTANDING THE OBJECTIVE

Priorities may be set during start-up from the command line or after processes have been started from the Task Manager. Six priority levels can be set from within Task Manager: realtime, high, above normal, normal, belownormal, and low.

WHAT YOU REALLY NEED TO KNOW

- The syntax to start a process from the command line is start/*<priority level>* *<process>*.
- You may change the priority of a process using Task Manager by right-clicking the process and then changing the priority.
- On multiprocessor machines, processes can be allocated to a specific processor with Task Manager by right-clicking the process and setting the affinity.
- Priorities cannot be set from the Performance Monitor, System Monitor, Services applet, or Event Viewer.
- To allocate system resources for an MS-DOS-based program, go to the Misc tab on the properties sheet for the program, and then select the amount of resources used for the program.

OBJECTIVES ON THE JOB

The two most common ways of changing priorities are through the Task Manager or from the command line. Typically, it is easier to change the priority through the Task Manager, thanks to its GUI environment.

PRACTICE TEST QUESTIONS

1. **You are running an instance of Access that needs an above normal priority. What is the command-line syntax used to start Access with this priority?**
   a. start /abovenormal msaccess.exe
   b. start /high msaccess.exe
   c. start /msaccess.exe above normal
   d. start /msaccess high
2. **You are currently running an application that should always have a low priority. Using Task Manager, you reduce the priority to low. The next time you start the application, with which priority will it start?**
   a. Low
   b. Normal
   c. Realtime
   d. High
3. **Which of the following is a method for forcing a 16-bit application to run in a separate address space? (Choose all that apply.)**
   a. Select Run in separate address space on the properties of the shortcut.
   b. On the command line, type start /<*application*> separate.
   c. On the command line, type start/separate <*application*>.
   d. On the command line, type separate/start <*application*>.
4. **What is the quickest way to determine whether your system has the recommended amount of available memory (greater than 4 MB)?**
   a. System Monitor
   b. Performance Monitor
   c. Task Manager, Process tab
   d. Task Manager, Performance tab
5. **Which tool should you use to monitor specific applications every 30 minutes for one week?**
   a. System Monitor
   b. Performance Monitor
   c. Network Monitor
   d. Event Viewer
6. **Which tool should you use to view the data obtained by monitoring the applications discussed in Question 5?**
   a. System Monitor
   b. Performance Monitor
   c. Network Monitor
   d. Event Viewer
7. **Once or twice per month, a certain third-party application runs wild and consumes all of the processor's resources. Can you set an alert on this process?**
   a. Yes
   b. No

OBJECTIVES

4.5 Start and stop processes

SETTING PROCESSES • STOPPING PROCESSES

UNDERSTANDING THE OBJECTIVE

Starting and stopping processes under Windows 2000 has not changed much from the same operations performed under Windows NT 4.0. You can still use the Task Manager to stop services, but two new priority-level options are available. The Services applet has been moved out of the Control Panel and into the Computer Management snap-in. The kill program, which was available in Windows NT 4.0, also works in Windows 2000 to stop programs that cannot be terminated in Task Manager. You may also start programs from the command line, as in Windows NT 4.0.

WHAT YOU REALLY NEED TO KNOW

- You can start a process from the command line by using the Start command.
- You can end a process from the command line by using the Kill utility.
- You can start a process in a shared address space or a separate address space.
- You can start a process with a specific priority by using the syntax start /<*priority*> process.
- You can specify an application to start as minimized or maximized.
- You may stop services in the Services applet, which is found within the computer Management snap-in.
- You can start 16-bit programs in their own address spaces to isolate them from one another. (All 16-bit programs start in the same NTVDM.) The syntax is start /separate <*process*>.

OBJECTIVES ON THE JOB

Some processes are not supposed to be stopped, such as lsass.exe, csrss.exe, and system. You can terminate these processes from the command line by using the Kill program, although this step may have detrimental effects on your system. You may also stop services with the Services applet. Stopping services in that way may affect other processes when they are stopped, however. Processes can also be set to start automatically or manually, or they can be disabled.

PRACTICE TEST QUESTIONS

1. **You want to stop the csrss.exe process through the Task Manager, but cannot. How can you stop this process?**
   a. Enter the Kill command on the command line.
   b. Enter the Stop command on the command line.
   c. Use the Services applet in the Control Panel.
   d. Use Process Manager in Computer Management.

2. **Ed, a co-worker, has been playing solitaire on his computer. He wants to start the program as minimized from the command line. Which command is used to accomplish this goal?**
   a. start sol.exe/min
   b. start sol.exe/minimized
   c. start min/ sol.exe
   d. start /min sol.exe

3. **What are the priority levels that may be assigned from the Task Manager, in the order from highest to lowest?**
   a. High, Normal, Low, Realtime
   b. Realtime, High, Normal, Low
   c. High, AboveNormal, Normal, BelowNormal, Low, Realtime
   d. Realtime, High, AboveNormal, Normal, BelowNormal, Low

4. **Which of the following can be used to start and stop services?**
   a. Services applet in Computer Management
   b. Task Management
   c. Service Management
   d. Performance Management

5. **Some processes can only be stopped by using the Kill command in the resource kit. What is the syntax to stop these processes?**
   a. kill <*process name | process ID*>
   b. kill <*process name*>
   c. kill <*process ID*>
   d. kill <*service name*>

6. **From within the Task Manager, you can sort processes based on greatest usage of the CPU.**
   a. True
   b. False

7. **Which of the following is a way to start the Task Manager? (Choose all that apply.)**
   a. Press Ctrl+Alt+Del and select Task Manager.
   b. Press Ctrl+Alt+Shft and select Task Manager.
   c. Right-click the taskbar and select Task Manager.
   d. Click Start, Run, and enter taskmgr.

OBJECTIVES

4.6 Optimize disk performance

OPTIMIZE DISK PERFORMANCE

UNDERSTANDING THE OBJECTIVE

Windows 2000 provides some of the same performance tools that existed in Windows NT 4.0, but adds other enhancements to assist network administrators. Among the new features in Windows 2000 are Quota Manager, Disk Defragmenter, and Disk Cleanup. You must format your drives as NTFS to use Quota Manager or Disk Compression. Disk Compression was available in Windows NT 4.0, as were the monitoring tools now found in Windows 2000.

WHAT YOU REALLY NEED TO KNOW

- Physical disk counters are enabled by default.
- Logical disk counters must be enabled manually. You can do this by typing diskperf – y at the command line.
- The Check Disk utility checks for file system errors and bad sectors.
- Disk Defragmenter analyzes or defragments your system. Run the analysis function to determine whether you really need to defragment your system.
- Disk Compression can be used to save space; you must format with NTFS to use it.
- Disk quotas can be used on NTFS partitions to limit users' home directories.
- Disk quotas are applied on a per-user, per-volume basis to the uncompressed size of the file.
- Any RAID level can be utilized by configuring your drives as dynamic drives during clean installations of Windows 2000.
- Mirroring and other levels of RAID may be used on systems that have been upgraded from Windows NT 4.0 and were in existence before the upgrade.

OBJECTIVES ON THE JOB

Network administrators have long asked for the ability to create quotas for users and to check for and defragment disks with native utilities. Although these utilities are available in Windows 2000, they come with limitations. Disk Defragmenter does not have the "set it and forget it" feature that can automatically run on a defined schedule. Quotas are limited by the fact that they work on a volume-by-volume basis. One enhancement allows you to set an alert, close Performance Monitor, and have the alert remain active.

PRACTICE TEST QUESTIONS

John configures a Windows 2000 Advanced Server that utilizes four processors, 1 GB RAM, and mirroring on the two 20 GB IDE dynamic disks, each of which contains two partitions. The boot and system files reside on the C drive, and users' home directories reside on the D drive.

1. **John sets up Performance Monitor to send you an alert if the current disk queue exceeds 10. Lately, this situation has been occurring more frequently. You have verified that the problem is not related to a lack of physical memory. How might John reduce the disk queue length? (Choose all that apply.)**
   a. Run Disk Defragmenter.
   b. Move the pagefile to the D: drive.
   c. Implement disk duplexing.
   d. Change the IDE drives to SCSI drives.
2. **After John reduces the queue length, the users are happy and response time improves. A few months later, however, users complain that it is taking a long time to access their home directories. The queue length averages 1.15. What would most likely solve this problem?**
   a. Move the pagefile to the D: drive.
   b. Run Disk Defragmenter.
   c. Add more RAM.
   d. Create a RAID 5 volume.
3. **John now thinks he has optimized the server but would like to monitor both the physical and logical disk counters. He can monitor the physical disks but not the logical disks. What must John do to be able to monitor the logical disk counters? (Choose all that apply.)**
   a. On the command line, enter diskperf.
   b. On the command line, enter diskperf – yv.
   c. Stop and start the disk subsystem service.
   d. Reboot the system.
4. **If John would like to have both fault tolerance and better read performance, how should he configure his server? (Choose all that apply.)**
   a. Add a third drive and create a RAID 5 volume.
   b. Create a striped volume on the two drives.
   c. Back up the system's data.
   d. Restore the system's data.
5. **Which utility or program will remove temporary Internet files from your server? (Choose all that apply.)**
   a. Internet Explorer
   b. Windows Explorer
   c. Disk Cleanup
   d. Disk Defragmenter

OBJECTIVES

4.7 Manage and optimize availability of System State data and end user data

SYSTEM STATE DATA • END USER DATA • MANAGE AVAILABILITY

UNDERSTANDING THE OBJECTIVE

Windows 2000 enhanced its backup capabilities by including an ability to back up not only to tape, but also to removable media, recordable CDs, and hard drives. Active Directory offers several restore levels, both authoritative and non-authoritative. You use the authoritative restore operation only if you want to restore items deleted from Active Directory. A non-authoritative restore operation allows other domain controllers to update Active Directory when the restoration has been completed.

WHAT YOU REALLY NEED TO KNOW

- The System State for all Windows 2000 machines consists of the Registry, the COM+ class registration database, and the boot files.
- System State data may include the Certificate Services database, if you are running certificate services.
- The System State includes the following, if the system is running on a domain controller: Active Directory service database and the SYSVOL directory.
- To complete an authoritative restore operation, you must run NTDUTIL after restoring the System State.
- You can use the Recovery Console to restore System State data.
- Five types of backups of user data are possible: Normal, Copy, Differential, Incremental, and Daily.
- Windows 2000 provides an option to exclude specific files such as the pagefile and log files.
- The Last Known Good Configuration boot option restores System State data saved at the last successful logon.
- The Directory Services Restore Mode boot option can rebuild and restore a damaged Active Directory.
- The optimization of the availability of the System State data and user data is simply a function of maintaining a system (or network) that is stable and reliable, while performing backups and procedures to restore damaged or lost data.

OBJECTIVES ON THE JOB

Windows 2000 has been greatly enhanced by the inclusion of a GUI interface and the ability to save to almost any type of media. Including the System State data in a backup is an easy way to save critical files. Don't rely on a single backup as your sole line of defense against data loss—provide other avenues of recovery. In addition, you should maintain multiple backups of all critical files and test your restoration procedures often.

PRACTICE TEST QUESTIONS

1. **System State data consists of which of the following on a Windows 2000 member server? (Choose all that apply.)**
   a. User database
   b. Registry
   c. COM+ registration database
   d. System boot files
2. **Which additional items are included in the System State? (Choose all that apply.)**
   a. SAM
   b. Active Directory services database
   c. SYSVOL directory
   d. WINNT/System32 subdirectory
3. **To restore the System State data to a domain controller that is part of a domain, and to have the other domain controllers update the restored data when it comes online, what type of restore operation should you use?**
   a. Non-authoritative restore
   b. Authoritative restore
   c. Domain restore
   d. SYSVOL
4. **You can create backups on which of the following? (Choose all that apply.)**
   a. Tape
   b. Recordable CDs
   c. Zip disks
   d. Hard drives
5. **You can back up specific components of the System State data instead of all of the components at once.**
   a. True
   b. False
6. **Which key must you press or command must you type to access the Directory Service Restore Mode menu item?**
   a. cmdcons
   b. restore /systemstate
   c. F8 at start-up
   d. rdisk
7. **Which type of backup of user data does not clear the archive attribute? (Choose all that apply.)**
   a. Normal
   b. Differential
   c. Incremental
   d. Copy

OBJECTIVES

4.8 Recover System State data and user data

SYSTEM STATE DATA • USER DATA RECOVERY • LKGC • ERD

UNDERSTANDING THE OBJECTIVE

Recovering System State data and user data is, at a minimum, a two-step process. You complete the first step—creating a backup or restoration path for the data—before any problems occur. You complete the second step only after a problem has occurred—namely, restoring the lost data from the backup.

WHAT YOU REALLY NEED TO KNOW

- System State data is protected in only three ways under Windows 2000: Last Known Good Configuration, Emergency Repair Disk, or a backup solution.
- The **LKGC** boots Windows 2000 using the state of the Registry recorded at the moment of the last successful logon. It is often a good first-step recovery technique after installing a bad driver or encountering a system that does not boot normally. See Objective 4.10.
- The ERD can be used in conjunction with the Setup boot floppies and the distribution CD to perform the Repair process, which can restore damaged files, restore some portions of the Registry, restore System State data, and even correct boot sector problems. You can also use the ERD through the Recovery Console as a source for files to copy back to their original, but damaged, locations (see Objective 4.11). *Note*: The ERD does not contain a complete copy of the Registry.
- A backup solution consists of any means by which data is copied from the storage devices of Windows 2000 onto another medium such as a tape, CD, floppy, or hard drive. The Windows 2000 Backup tool, and many other Windows 2000-specific tools, can back up in-memory System State data when the backup is performed. This System State data may be used in a restore process and thereby return the system to its configuration at the time of the backup procedure. See Objective 4.9.
- Manual backups of the %systemroot%\repair directory can provide you with backups to the Registry. They can be used to restore all or part of the Registry through one of the Registry editing tools.

OBJECTIVES ON THE JOB

Eternal vigilance is the only way to protect data created on your network and used to support your network. In most cases, last week's backup is not good enough. You need to discover which level of protection matches the value, timeliness, and importance of both your System State data and user data, then adjust your protection strategies and schedules accordingly.

PRACTICE TEST QUESTIONS

1. **Which of the following actions is the best first step to take when attempting to restore a system that no longer boots?**
    a. Reinstall Windows 2000.
    b. Use the Repair process.
    c. Use the Recovery Console to restore files.
    d. Restore the system from backup.
2. **How is the Last Known Good Configuration accessed?**
    a. From the Processes tab of the Task Manager
    b. By holding down the left Shift key during start-up
    c. By pressing F8 during the boot menu
    d. Through the Shutdown command from the Start menu
3. **You log on to your Windows 2000 system as the Administrator (logon session A) and then install a new device driver. The process requests that you reboot the system. After the reboot (logon session B), the screen appears distorted, but you are able to log system reports and errors. You decide to invoke the Last Known Good Configuration. To which saved System State does the system return?**
    a. That saved at logon session A
    b. That saved at logon session B
4. **What would have been a better choice of action in the scenario described in Question 3?**
    a. Use a Registry Editor to restore the System State data instead of using LKGC.
    b. Install the old video drivers over the damaged/corrupted drivers during logon session B.
    c. Don't log on the second time before invoking the LKGC.
    d. Manually delete the video driver files.
5. **Which of the following is a required element during the Repair process? (Choose all that apply.)**
    a. Emergency Repair Disk
    b. Distribution CD
    c. Installed Recovery Console
    d. Setup boot floppies
    e. An administrative password
6. **The Windows 2000 Backup tool can save System State data to the backup media along with user data.**
    a. True
    b. False
7. **Which of the following would be useful in performing a complete Registry restoration?**
    a. Emergency Repair Disk
    b. Distribution CD
    c. Logging on as a Service user
    d. Manual backup of the \repair directory

OBJECTIVES

4.9 Recover System State data by using Windows Backup

SYSTEM STATE DATA • USER DATA RECOVERY • LKGC • ERD

UNDERSTANDING THE OBJECTIVE

Windows 2000 has a native backup utility, which you can use to provide backup protection of user data, System State data, and other files stored on the computer.

WHAT YOU REALLY NEED TO KNOW

- System State data can be backed up only from the local system; Windows 2000 Backup is not capable of capturing System State data from other systems over the network.
- You can schedule the Windows 2000 Backup utility. Backups can be restored to their original locations or to alternative locations, or all files can be deposited in a single directory (losing the original directory structure). When you are restoring files, if versions of the backed-up files exist in the restore location, you have three options: do not replace any existing files, replace a file only if the existing file is older than the backed-up file, and always replace the file.
- Backups can be performed at the command line or through batch files using the ntbackup command. Restores can be performed only through the GUI interface.
- Backup offers five types of backups: Normal, Copy, Daily, Incremental, and Differential.
- When you are restoring System State data to a domain controller, NTDSUTIL can be used to force other domain controllers to accept the restored data.

OBJECTIVES ON THE JOB

The Windows 2000 Backup utility is a fully functional backup solution, sufficient to protect a single system. It can save any file on any storage device both locally and from any accessible network share, including custom and hidden/admin shares (that is, those with a trailing $ created by the system automatically upon start-up). Maintaining regular backups is the only way to ensure that data recovery can be performed. Without a backup, no recovery option is available in the event of loss or significant corruption.

PRACTICE TEST QUESTIONS

1. **Which types of data can Windows 2000 Backup save to backup media? (Choose all that apply.)**
   a. Local System State data
   b. System State data from other systems on the network
   c. Local data files
   d. Data files from other systems on the network
2. **Which of the following strategies provides you with 100% backup coverage of your Windows 2000 system, is the most efficient in terms of overall backup time, and consumes the least amount of backup media (that is, the number of backup tapes)?**
   a. A Copy backup of all files on a daily basis
   b. A Daily backup every 12 hours
   c. A Normal backup once every two weeks, with an Incremental backup daily
   d. A Normal backup once every two weeks, with a Differential backup daily
   e. A Normal backup once every two weeks, with a Daily backup each day
3. **Match the following statements with one or more of the five backup types. Assume that the backup set consists of all possible files on the local hard drive.**
   1. Creates copy of every selected file every time it is used
   2. Resets the archive bit
   3. Captures all files changed within the last 25 hours (assuming no other backup has occurred in that time period)
   4. Copies only files changed since the last backup
   5. The best option for work-in-progress backups to removable media
   6. When used following a Normal backup on a daily basis, provides a means to restore an entire system using only two backup media sets

   a. Normal
   b. Copy
   c. Daily
   d. Incremental
   e. Differential
4. **Backup and restore operations can be performed at the command line or through batch files using the ntbackup command.**
   a. True
   b. False
5. **Which of the following statements are true?**
   a. Restoring system data to a non-domain controller requires the use of NTDSUTIL.
   b. Restoring system data to a domain controller requires the use of NTDSUTIL.
   c. NTDSUTIL should be used on a domain controller to force other domain controllers to accept the restored data.
   d. NTDSUTIL should be used on a domain controller to allow the local domain controller to accept changes and overwrites to the locally restored data.

OBJECTIVES

4.10 Troubleshoot system restoration by starting in safe mode

SAFE MODE

UNDERSTANDING THE OBJECTIVE

The advanced boot options of Windows 2000 offer the ability to circumvent nonessential installed components to restore a system to normal operation.

WHAT YOU REALLY NEED TO KNOW

- The boot menu includes the following options:

  Safe Mode—boot with minimal drivers and system files (VGA, mouse, keyboard, storage, and essential services, but no network support)

  Safe Mode with Networking—safe mode with non-PC Card network support

  Safe Mode with Command Prompt—safe mode with command prompt, not GUI

  Enable Boot Logging—turns on recording of loaded drivers to NTBTLOG.TXT

  Enable VGA Mode—turns on minimal VGA support for non-safe mode start-ups (640 x 480 resolutions with 256 or 16 colors)

  Last Known Good Configuration—boots using the Registry status saved at the moment of the last successful logon

  Directory Services Restore Mode (Windows 2000 domain controllers only)—rebuilds the Active Directory

  Debugging Mode—transmits debugging and boot progress data over the serial port to be captured by a second system (see the Windows 2000 Resource Kit)
- Use safe mode when a bad video driver has been installed and the LKGC does not remedy the situation. While in safe mode, you should be able to reset the video settings. This process can also be used for any nonessential driver or system file failure.
- You can use safe mode with networking on any system not using a PC Card or PCMCIA NICs for network access. This boot method should be used when the required installation or driver files are accessible only over the network.
- Use safe mode with command prompt when you need to peform basic file manipulation options and when the GUI accessed through safe mode fails to offer a functioning environment.

OBJECTIVES ON THE JOB

Safe mode provides system administrators with a possible window of hope when bad drivers are installed on the system or existing drivers become damaged or deleted. Without safe mode, reinstalling Windows 2000 would be an all-too-frequent remedy.

PRACTICE TEST QUESTIONS

1. **You have installed a new video card. To install the drivers, you use a vendor-supplied setup utility. After rebooting, the screen is so scrambled that you can't read anything. You press Ctrl+Alt+Del, type in your password, and press Enter. The screen is still too distorted to read anything, determine the location of icons, or find the location of the cursor. Which of the following is a valid option to restore the system's video? (Choose all that apply.)**
   a. Boot using the Last Known Good Configuration.
   b. Boot using safe mode.
   c. Boot using safe mode with command prompt.
   d. Boot using Directory Services restore mode.
2. **Using a different computer from that described in Question 1, you visit the vendor's Web site. You discover that the drivers shipped with the product were damaged during duplication. New functioning drivers are available for download, and you retrieve and copy them to a floppy. The instructions state that the best method for installing the drivers is to manually replace the files already present on the system. Into which mode should you boot to perform this operation?**
   a. Directory Services Restore Mode
   b. Safe Mode with Command Prompt
   c. Debugging Mode
   d. No mode will enable this process
3. **When using an advanced boot option, such as safe mode, logging on (at least to the local system) is still required.**
   a. True
   b. False
4. **Safe mode can be used to repair or correct which of the following problems? (Choose all that apply.)**
   a. A malfunctioning keyboard
   b. A damaged security service
   c. A deleted network protocol driver
   d. A damaged video driver
   e. A lost password
   f. Failed installation of Active Directory
   g. Corrupted driver for an external tape backup device
   h. Registry corruption
5. **If the core Windows GUI driver files become corrupted, which boot method might you use to access important data files on the system before performing a complete reinstallation of Windows 2000?**
   a. Safe Mode
   b. Safe Mode with Networking
   c. Safe Mode with Command Prompt
   d. Last Known Good Configuration

OBJECTIVES

4.11 Recover System State data by using the Recovery Console

RECOVERY CONSOLE

UNDERSTANDING THE OBJECTIVE

The Recovery Console is a command-line interface that grants Administrators access to all files and folders on a Windows 2000 system. From within the Recovery Console, the user can access any file on any local volume (FAT, FAT32, or NTFS). By using special commands, you can also perform some Registry management by enabling or disabling services and drivers.

WHAT YOU REALLY NEED TO KNOW

- The Recovery Console is a native component of Windows 2000, but it is not installed by default.
- The Recovery Console is a command-line interface through which you can execute recovery attempts. These attempts can consist of replacing files (driver, system, and Registry files), enabling/disabling services and drivers, formatting hard drives, repairing boot sectors, and performing file operations (copy, move, rename, delete, and so on).
- You must log on as the Administrator to use the Recovery Console.
- In the Recovery Console, corrupted, damaged, and deleted files can be replaced from backups stored on local hard drives or from local removable media (floppies or CDs). You can also disable or enable services and/or drivers that may be hampering the system's normal operation. If you have a backup of the Registry files available, you can replace them in the \repair directory.
- By default, the Recovery Console is configured to prevent writing of files to floppies or other removable media. This choice can be altered by enabling the Recovery Console: Allow Floppy Copy and Access to All Files and All Folders security option from the **LCP**.

OBJECTIVES ON THE JOB

The Recovery Console is not a miracle worker; it's a command-line-only, minimal operating system that can manipulate files, folders, and the Registry of a Windows 2000 system. The Recovery Console is both a blessing and a curse—you must be familiar with the commands and the files you are manipulating to effect a solution for a failed system.

PRACTICE TEST QUESTIONS

1. **Which of the following situations would most likely be a candidate for attempted repair through the Recovery Console? (Choose all that apply.)**
   a. A hard drive used to store data has stopped responding to the system
   b. A user account has been locked out of the domain
   c. A newly installed driver prevents the system from booting
   d. A boot sector has become damaged
   e. Registry files have become corrupted
   f. A nonessential service is consuming 100% of the CPU's resources
   g. An IRQ conflict occurs with a newly installed NIC
2. **Which method is used to gain access to the Recovery Console? (Choose all that apply.)**
   a. Use the Advanced Boot options menu after the Recovery Console is installed.
   b. Elect to boot into the Recovery Console from the Shutdown command.
   c. Execute cmdcons from the Run command.
   d. Use the Setup boot disks.
3. **The Recovery Console is installed on Windows 2000 Server systems by default.**
   a. True
   b. False
4. **Which of the following statements is true about the Recovery Console? (Choose all that apply.)**
   a. It grants access to all partitions formatted with FAT, FAT32, or NTFS.
   b. New software can be installed.
   c. New user accounts can be created.
   d. You must log on with the Administrator user account.
   e. The Registry can be restored by overwriting files in the \repair directory.
   f. By default, files can be copied to removable media.
   g. Both services and drivers can be enabled and disabled.
5. **Which action must be performed to install the Recovery Console?**
   a. Use the Add/Remove Programs applet.
   b. Execute winnt32 /cmdcons.
   c. Install Windows 2000 Advanced Server.
   d. Execute MAKEDISK from the distribution CD.
6. **Which feature of the Recovery Console can be managed through the Local Computer Policy? (Choose all that apply.)**
   a. Allow floppy copy and access to all files and all folders.
   b. Restrict access to NTFS volumes.
   c. Automatically log on to the Administrator account.
   d. Decrypt the security database.

Section 5

Managing, Configuring, and Troubleshooting Storage Use

OBJECTIVES

5.1 Configure disks and volumes

BASIC AND DYNAMIC DISKS • DISK REGION • DISK GROUPS • DATABASE

UNDERSTANDING THE OBJECTIVE

Whether you intend to set up Windows 2000 Server as a stand-alone system or as part of an enterprise environment, effective configuration of disks is critical if the integrity and accessibility of the data stored on them are to be maintained. Therefore, it is essential to have a meticulous understanding of the concepts involved in creating an effective disk strategy so that your network will run smoothly and without incident.

WHAT YOU REALLY NEED TO KNOW

- Windows 2000, unlike Windows NT 4.0, supports two disk configurations: basic disks and dynamic disks.
- Basic disks can contain primary, extended, and logical partitions.
- Dynamic disks are new and exclusive to Windows 2000 and bring enhanced and logical partitions.
- Dynamic disks also offer enhanced functionality, such as the ability to effect disk configuration changes without requiring a system reboot.
- Dynamic disks store configuration data in a 1 MB region at the end of the disk. They can be divided into areas called volumes, similar to partitions in basic disks.
- Another feature unique to dynamic disks is a Disk Group, which is a group of disks managed as a whole that assists in disk management and helps avert data loss.
- Seven dynamic disk volume types exist: simple, spanned, striped, mirrored, **RAID 5**, boot, and system volumes. In Microsoft terminology, the boot volume holds the system files and the system volume contains the boot files.
- Windows 2000 disks are managed by the Disk Management snap-in for the **MMC**, which connects to the Logical Disk Manager service. Both local and remote disks can be administered via this snap-in.
- New disks that are added to a machine must be initialized before use. Failure to do so will result in the inability to configure partitions/volumes on the disk. When you initialize the disk, select the basic or dynamic disks option as required.

OBJECTIVES ON THE JOB

When moving a disk from one computer to another, you must select Rescan Disks from the Action menu in the Disk Management snap-in. To import a collection of disks (or part of that group) from another system (marked Foreign), right-click the group and choose Import Foreign Disks.

PRACTICE TEST QUESTIONS

1. **You are a junior trainee Administrator at a company and have been given a preconfigured Windows 2000 Professional laptop computer for use on your network. You want to upgrade the basic disk configuration to dynamic disks, but your attempt fails. What is the problem?**
   a. Dynamic disks are not supported on laptops.
   b. You haven't initialized the disk before trying to upgrade it to a dynamic disk.
   c. A local policy prohibits this action.
   d. You need to add another PC Card hard drive to the laptop to take advantage of the benefits of dynamic disks.

2. **You are the domain Administrator at a software company and want to convert a hard disk completely full of data to a dynamic disk to take advantage of spanned volumes. When you attempt this procedure, it fails. Why?**
   a. You need to initialize the disk.
   b. The disk is formatted as FAT32 and needs to be NTFS.
   c. The region at the end of the disk has insufficient free space to hold the volume information.
   d. You cannot convert basic disks that already contain data to dynamic disks.

3. **Susie, a software developer, works on a multi-disk, multi-boot computer. She recently added, for application testing purposes, another disk with Windows 2000 Server installed. She cannot access this volume from the other operating systems on her computer. Why?**
   a. Dynamic disks are only supported in Windows 2000.
   b. Susie needs to convert the Windows 2000 Server disk to dynamic.
   c. Susie needs to convert the other disks in her computer to dynamic.
   d. The Windows 2000 Server file system needs to be FAT16 or FAT32.

4. **You have a Windows 2000 Server machine configured with five hard disks. One hard disk is used for the boot and system volumes. The other four hard disks are used for data storage and are configured as a striped volume. All disks are dynamic. Management has issued a policy directive that states that all data stored on the company's hard disks must be fault tolerant, while minimizing disk usage. What must you do?**
   a. Nothing, the present configuration is fault tolerant.
   b. Back up the data on the striped volume, configure the four disks as a RAID 5 volume, and restore the data.
   c. Back up the data on the striped volume, configure the four disks as a mirror volume, and restore the data.
   d. Convert the existing striped volume to a RAID 5 volume using the Disk Management snap-in in the MMC.

OBJECTIVES

5.2 Monitor disks and volumes

COUNTERS • ALERTS • OBSERVATION

UNDERSTANDING THE OBJECTIVE

The monitoring of disks and volumes constitutes an important aspect of Windows 2000 system management and needs careful and close attention. You must keep track of numerous things in Windows 2000 disk systems to attain and maintain optimum disk performance, ranging from the level of disk utilization to the cadence of the disk's transfer capacity, the quantity of disk usage, and the formation of a queue for the disk system. Moreover, it is vital to monitor disk operations, which can take the form of interrupts and paging activity, because these activities can dramatically affect other system resources, such as memory and processors.

WHAT YOU REALLY NEED TO KNOW

- The three primary built-in Windows 2000 tools for disk monitoring are Task Manager, Performance Logs and Alerts, and System Monitor.
- System Monitor utilizes counters to monitor both logical and physical disks. Physical disk counters are activated by default. To monitor logical disks, you must run the diskperf—yv command from the command line.
- To perform disk monitoring, begin by setting up a performance baseline using System Monitor. This baseline should include disk counters and a selection of other system resource counters to establish a balanced baseline.
- You can determine whether a genuine disk bottleneck exists by assessing a combination of factors, including the presence of a steady rate of disk activity that exceeds your baseline by a significant margin, unrelenting disk queue lengths that remain higher than the value of 2, and a lack of insignificant paging. Without this combination of events, the problem likely lies elsewhere in the system.
- Avg. Disk Queue Length, Disk Reads/sec, Disk Writes/sec, Memory\Pages/sec, Memory\Page, Reads/sec Memory\Page, and Writes/sec are all counters that you can examine when you suspect that paging might overburden the system.

OBJECTIVES ON THE JOB

If a disk is running low on disk space, consider running Disk Cleanup or implementing Remote Storage for infrequently accessed data. You can store this data on virtual disks such as tape drives or optical storage and then retrieve it as necessary. If you are running NTFS on your volumes, then disk quotas might be a feasible option to limit users' disk space usage.

PRACTICE TEST QUESTIONS

1. **You are trying to monitor logical disk counters for your disk system on a Windows 2000 Server, but are unable to do so. You have enabled the logical disk counters. What is the most likely cause of your problem?**
   a. You did not restart the machine.
   b. You did not enable the physical disk counters.
   c. You have no logical disks configured on the system.
   d. The Disk System Service is disabled by default and must be started before you can monitor logical disk counters.
2. **After installing a Windows 2000 network at your company, you want to establish a performance baseline to use when monitoring disk activity on your disk systems. When and how should you establish this baseline?**
   a. Immediately after setting up the new network, establish the baseline by recording data at regular intervals throughout the day and over periods of time, such as daily, weekly, and monthly.
   b. Once the new network has settled into a consistent and routine state, establish the baseline by recording data at regular intervals throughout the day and over periods of time, such as daily, weekly, and monthly.
   c. There is no need to establish a baseline; Windows 2000 automatically monitors and optimizes the disk systems over which it has control.
   d. Immediately after setting up the new network, establish the baseline by recording data for an hour.
3. **You suspect that the excessive disk activity on one of your hard disks might be caused by a lack of memory. Which disk counters should you monitor to determine whether paging is the source of the problem?**
   a. Memory counters only
   b. Disk counters only
   c. Memory and disk counters
   d. Memory and processor counters
4. **You are concerned about disk fragmentation on your physical disks, which are located remotely. How could you learn about of any disk fragmentation that occurs?**
   a. This type of monitoring is not possible.
   b. Windows 2000 does not provide this functionality by default; use the SENDALER.EXE Resource Kit utility instead.
   c. Set up an alert that is triggered when the Split IO/sec counter exceeds a specified threshold.
   d. Set up an alert that is triggered when the Fragments/sec counter exceeds a specified threshold.

OBJECTIVES

5.3 Troubleshoot disks and volumes

DIAGNOSE • STATUS • RECOVERY

UNDERSTANDING THE OBJECTIVE

You must be familiar with the fundamentals of disk management to be an effective troubleshooter when working with Windows 2000 disk systems. Windows 2000 provides the Administrator with a plethora of information from which to diagnose and swiftly resolve disk problems. Understanding this material is key to maintaining disk systems with minimal downtime.

WHAT YOU REALLY NEED TO KNOW

- Windows 2000 displays disk status descriptions in Disk Management. These descriptions follow:
  - Online: The disk is functioning correctly with no known errors. This status is displayed for basic and dynamic disks.
  - Online (Errors): A disk displaying this status has **I/O** errors. If the I/O errors are transient, you can use the Reactivate Disk command to restore the disk's online status. This status is displayed for dynamic disks only.
  - Offline: An inaccessible disk is either corrupted or sporadically available. This status is displayed for dynamic disks only.
  - Foreign: The disk has been moved from another computer but is not yet imported into the new host system. This status is displayed for dynamic disks only.
  - Unreadable: The disk is inaccessible, most likely due to I/O errors, corruption, or hardware failure; possibly the disk configuration database may be damaged. Both basic and dynamic disks can display this status.
  - Unrecognized: The disk has an OEM signature (for example, a UNIX disk) and **DM** does not permit its use. Only unrecognized disks display this status.
  - No Media: This status is displayed only for CD-ROM and removable disk drives when no media is actually present in the drive.

OBJECTIVES ON THE JOB

You can bring offline disks back online by using the Reactivate Disks and/or Remove Disk command. With the latter option, you must delete any volumes (or mirrors) on the disk before performing this operation. To preserve the mirror rather than deleting the whole volume, you may remove the mirror first. If a dynamic disk is displaying the Unreadable status, the likely cause is I/O errors or corruption on a portion of the disk. Running the Rescan Disks command may bring the disk back online. To add a disk marked as Foreign to your system, run the Import Foreign Disks command.

PRACTICE TEST QUESTIONS

1. **What does the Healthy (At Risk) volume status description mean?**
   a. The disk is corrupt, but the volume is accessible.
   b. The disk is corrupt, and the volume is inaccessible.
   c. The disk contains I/O errors, but the volume is accessible.
   d. The disk contains I/O errors, and the volume is not accessible.
2. **What does the Failed Redundancy (At Risk) volume status description mean?**
   a. The partition contains I/O errors, but the data is accessible.
   b. The volume contains I/O errors, and the data is inaccessible.
   c. The data on a basic partition is no longer fault tolerant, and the underlying disk contains I/O errors.
   d. The data on a dynamic volume is no longer fault tolerant, and the underlying disk contains I/O errors.
3. **A disk in your Windows 2000 Server is displaying its status as Online (Errors). What does this status mean?**
   a. The disk is fragmented.
   b. The disk needs formatting.
   c. The disk contains I/O errors.
   d. The disk's spin speed setting is incorrect.
4. **Disk Management shows a RAID 5 volume's status as Failed Redundancy. What does this status mean?**
   a. The volume has lost its fault tolerance, and the data is inaccessible.
   b. The volume is healthy; this status is the default.
   c. The volume is still fault tolerant, and the data is inaccessible.
   d. The volume has lost its fault tolerance, but the data is accessible.
5. **You have just inserted a new disk into your removable disk drive on your Windows 2000 Server. The disk's status is No Media. What is the most likely explanation for this status?**
   a. The removable disk is faulty, and you must replace it with another one.
   b. You have not executed the Rescan Disks command to bring the removable disk online.
   c. Windows 2000 Server does not support removable disks.
   d. You need to press F5 to refresh the disk configuration.
6. **Disk Management reports the status of a new disk taken from another server that you recently installed in your Windows 2000 Server as Unrecognized. How can you explain this status?**
   a. The disk contains an OEM signature from another system, such as UNIX.
   b. The disk has not been formatted.
   c. The Rescan Disk command has not been run in Disk Management.
   d. The Import Foreign Disk command needs to be executed in Disk Management.

OBJECTIVES

5.4 Configure data compression

COMPRESS • ION • DISK USAGE

UNDERSTANDING THE OBJECTIVE

Windows 2000 includes support for data compression on volumes, folders, and individual files. Data compression is useful when you have limited disk space. Note, however, that compression is better suited to Windows 2000 Professional than to Windows 2000 Server, especially when servers have heavy write traffic, as file system performance can be severely degraded by compression.

WHAT YOU REALLY NEED TO KNOW

- Any Windows program can read and write to Windows 2000 compressed files without the files first requiring decompression by another utility. This ability provides seamless operability.
- Windows 2000 data compression is supported only on NTFS volumes—not on FAT16 and FAT32 volumes.
- Compressed files cannot be encrypted—an important consideration.
- The Resource Kit contains some useful command-line utilities: compress, expand, and diruse (provides information on the actual disk space used by compressed files on NTFS volumes).
- Moving a compressed or uncompressed file or folder to another folder on an NTFS volume always preserves the file's or folder's original attributes, irrespective of whether the target folder is compressed.
- Compressed or uncompressed files or folders that are copied to another folder on an NTFS volume inherit the attributes of the target folder, whether it is compressed or not.
- Compressed or uncompressed files or folders that are copied from a FAT volume to a folder on an NTFS volume inherit the target folder's attributes.
- Compressed files or folders that are moved or copied to a FAT volume are automatically decompressed, as compression is not supported on the volume type.

OBJECTIVES ON THE JOB

Configuring compression on Windows 2000 volumes, folders, and files is simple from the GUI. If subfolders and files exist, you must decide whether to compress them as well. You can display compressed files and folders in a different color in Windows Explorer.

PRACTICE TEST QUESTIONS

1. **Your compressed files are highlighted in a different color in Windows Explorer on your Windows 2000 Server. When you encrypt these compressed files, they are no longer highlighted in blue. Why?**
    a. Windows 2000 files and folders cannot posses the compression and encryption attributes at the same time.
    b. You need to reboot the server before the files will be displayed in a different color.
    c. This action is impossible; you cannot encrypt compressed files without first decompressing them.
    d. When Windows 2000 files are marked with the compression and encryption attributes, they are always displayed with the standard Windows Explorer color.
2. **You copy a compressed file to an uncompressed folder on an NTFS volume. What compression attribute does the transferred file acquire?**
    a. Read only
    b. Uncompressed
    c. Compressed
    d. Read only and System
3. **You move an uncompressed file on a FAT32 volume to a compressed folder. What compression attribute does the transferred file acquire?**
    a. Compressed
    b. Hidden
    c. System
    d. Uncompressed
4. **You move some compressed files to a folder on a FAT32 volume. What compression attribute does the transferred files acquire?**
    a. Compressed
    b. Hidden
    c. System
    d. Uncompressed
5. **You are trying to compress some files on a volume on your Windows 2000 Server. The Advanced button is not visible on the General tab of the files' properties sheet. Why?**
    a. The files are encrypted; you cannot compress encrypted files.
    b. The files reside on a FAT16 or FAT32 volume.
    c. The Advanced button appears on the Compression tab in the files' properties sheet.
    d. You cannot compress individual files on a volume.
6. **When compressed files are copied, whether it is over a network or on the same computer, they are decompressed, copied, and then recompressed again (providing that the target folder is compressed).**
    a. True
    b. False

OBJECTIVES

5.5 Configure disk quotas

DISK QUOTAS

UNDERSTANDING THE OBJECTIVE

Disk quotas, which were possible only with third-party products in Windows NT 4.0, are natively supported in Windows 2000. They offer real benefits to systems administrators who seek to control or track users' disk usage. To maximize the value offered by disk quotas, you should understand the topic of quota configuration fully.

WHAT YOU REALLY NEED TO KNOW

- ◆ Disk quotas can be set only on NTFS volumes—not on FAT16 or FAT32 volumes. Quotas cannot be set on individual folders, but rather on an entire volume. You can divide a disk into multiple volumes, each of which has a different quota limit, if a per-user policy is not in force.
- ◆ You can configure quotas both locally and remotely.
- ◆ The Quota Entries dialog provides several options, such as the Find command and the ability to sort quota entries by various criteria. In addition, quota settings on volumes can be imported and/or exported, which simplifies and streamlines configuration.
- ◆ Quotas are based on file ownership. If a user takes ownership of files, that change affects the user's disk space usage under disk quotas.
- ◆ If a user moves files from one folder to another, no change in his or her disk space usage occurs. If the user copies all of his or her files to another directory on the same volume, it will double the user's disk usage.
- ◆ Irrespective of whether a volume spans one or many disks, the quota limit on that volume remains the same for a particular user. Furthermore, if a volume contains multiple directories to which a user saves data, it makes no difference to a user's quota limit; the threshold applies to the volume as a whole.
- ◆ You can delete a user's quotas from the Quota Entries dialog box, but only when the user's files have been deleted, been moved, or their ownership has changed.
- ◆ Users can exceed their quota limits if the Deny disk space to users exceeding quota limit option is left unchecked on the Quota tab.

OBJECTIVES ON THE JOB

Consider the effects of introducing disk quotas into your network environment before you actually implement this scenario. You should take into account your users' needs and allow for expansion, although it is probably best to start your users with reasonably low disk quota levels and increase them as a percentage of the original figure as required. You may also audit your users' disk usage before putting a disk quota policy into force, thereby better gauging their requirements.

PRACTICE TEST QUESTIONS

1. **You are trying to set up disk quotas on a Windows 2000 machine, but the Quota tab is missing. Why?**
   a. You need to be a member of the Quota Creators group to implement disk quotas.
   b. You need to be a member of the Server Operators group to implement disk quotas.
   c. You need to be a member of the Power Users group to implement disk quotas.
   d. The volume is formatted as FAT32.
2. **You inherited a machine with an NTFS volume and now want to configure disk quotas on a per-user basis for it. The Quota tab is nowhere to be found. Why?**
   a. Quotas can be applied only to FAT16 and FAT32 volumes.
   b. You are not a member of the Power Users group.
   c. You do not have administrative privileges.
   d. You are not a member of the Quota Creators group.
3. **You configured disk quotas on a per-user basis in your 2000-user Windows 2000 network. David recently left the company, and you want to locate and delete his quota entry. You use the Find command in the Quota Entries dialog. Which parameter can you employ to find David's entry? (Choose all that apply.)**
   a. domain_name\user_name
   b. user_name@domain_name
   c. domain_name@user_name
   d. user_name\domain_name
4. **Sue, a user, has a quota limit of 50 MB on an NTFS volume and has stored six 5 MB files on this volume. She copies three of these files to another directory on the same volume. What will be her disk space usage now?**
   a. 40 MB
   b. 45 MB
   c. 50 MB
   d. Sue's disk space usage is unchanged.

OBJECTIVES

5.6 Monitor disk quotas

DOCUMENT • AUDIT • LOG

UNDERSTANDING THE OBJECTIVE

No only do you have the capability to restrict users' disk space usage with disk quotas, but you can also monitor or audit that practice (or both) without limiting users' disk space consumption. Having a comprehensive understanding of this aspect of disk quotas will ensure that your network enjoys efficient disk space usage and optimal user utilization of that space.

WHAT YOU REALLY NEED TO KNOW

- You can track and document users' disk space utilization without enforcing any limits on those users.
- Enabling disk quotas has a slight drawback, in that it increases server overhead. You can enable disk quotas to perform a network audit of disk usage only, thereby maintaining the normal performance of your file servers.
- If you select the Deny disk space to users exceeding quota limit option on the Quota tab, users exceeding their prescribed limits will receive an "insufficient disk space" warning message.
- If you select the Log event when a user exceeds their quota limit option on the Quota tab, a record will be written to the System Log whenever users breach the predefined limit. This record can then be viewed in Event Viewer using filters.
- You can create quota reports on a per-user basis by clicking on single or multiple entries in the Quota Entries dialog and then dragging those entries into an Excel spreadsheet or Word document. The data transferred is preserved in the same format as it was displayed in the Quota Entries dialog.
- Three disk quota states exist: quota disabled, usage neither tracked nor enforced (the default state); quota and usage tracked, but disk limits not enforced; and quota enforced, usage tracked, and disk limits enforced.

OBJECTIVES ON THE JOB

You can maintain a chronological record of your users' disk space usage by documenting disk space usage on a per-user basis. You can use this information to highlight additional disk space requirements for your network. Disk space auditing on a per-user basis also shows the distribution of the disk space for any particular user. Armed with this knowledge, you can inform users of disk space overuse or increase their disk space limits, if the quota enforced state is in place. Moreover, the ability to create reports on disk space utilization can provide senior management in any given organization with the black-and-white statistics they may need.

PRACTICE TEST QUESTIONS

1. **If event logging is enabled for disk quotas, where is the event logged?**
    a. Windows Quota Log
    b. Windows Application Log
    c. Windows Security Log
    d. Windows System Log
2. **You can export user information from the Quota Entries dialog to a commadelimited file that can be imported into applications such as Microsoft Excel.**
    a. True
    b. False
3. **Management asked you to provide a comprehensive report detailing the disk space utilization of all users within your organization. Which program can you use to provide this information? (Choose all that apply.)**
    a. Microsoft Word
    b. Microsoft WordPad
    c. Microsoft Excel
    d. Microsoft Notepad
4. **You are the network administrator for a software company. Recently, you noticed that the amount of free disk space is decreasing. You suspect that some users are using disk space excessively—not in line with corporate policy. Which disk quota statistic would be appropriate to identify the errant users?**
    a. Quota disabled
    b. Quota tracked
    c. Quota enforced
    d. Quota monitored
5. **You want to track users' disk space usage without enforcing any disk space limits on those users. In addition, you want to keep a record of whenever a user surpasses a predefined warning level and disk space limit. Which settings should you use?**
    a. On the Quota tab, select the check box for Deny disk space to users exceeding quota limit.
    b. On the Quota tab, deselect the check box for Deny disk space to users exceeding quota limit.
    c. On the Quota tab, select the check box for Deny disk space to users exceeding quota limit. Enable the Log event when a user exceeds their warning level and Log event when a user exceeds their quota limit settings.
    d. On the Quota tab, select the check box for Deny disk space to users exceeding quota limit. Enable the Log event when a user exceeds their quota limit setting.

OBJECTIVES

5.7 Recover from disk failures

MONITOR • REPAIR • COMMAND

UNDERSTANDING THE OBJECTIVE

Disk failure recovery is a challenging topic that requires due diligence to keep your Windows 2000 disk system running with minimal downtime. Many recovery scenarios are possible with Windows 2000 disk systems, so you need to use the correct procedure for any particular configuration. Furthermore, you should know whether your system includes basic or dynamic disks, as this factor will influence the type of recovery method you employ.

WHAT YOU REALLY NEED TO KNOW

- To recover from a basic mirrored volume failure, execute the Repair Volume command. If this effort fails, run the Resynchronize Mirror command to bring the disk back online.
- To recover from a dynamic mirrored volume failure when the volume's status is Failed Redundancy and the disk's status is Offline or Online (Errors), execute the Reactivate Disk command after checking the disk's connections.
- If you cannot bring a dynamic volume's status back to Healthy by running the Reactivate Disk command, rebuild the mirror on another dynamic disk.
- If DM reports that a RAID 5 array's volume status is Failed Redundancy and the disk's status is Online, try to repair the volume by issuing the Repair Volume command. If this effort fails, try running the Regenerate Parity command to restore fault tolerance.
- To recover from a dynamic RAID 5 volume failure when the volume's status is Failed Redundancy and the disk's status is Offline or Online (Errors), execute the Reactivate Disk command after checking the disk's connections. If this effort fails to bring the volume's status back to Healthy, issue the Repair Volume command.
- When repairing mirror and RAID 5 volumes because of disk failures, you must match the new disk's type to that of the disk being repaired. Do not mix basic and dynamic disks in mirror and RAID 5 volumes.

OBJECTIVES ON THE JOB

Aside from ensuring that the disk types are the same when you repair fault-tolerant volumes, you should verify that sufficient free disk space is available on a new disk to rebuild a mirror or RAID 5 volume. Otherwise, DM will not make commands available. Many potential catastrophes can be warded off through effective disk maintenance.

PRACTICE TEST QUESTIONS

1. **Two 20 GB dynamic hard disks are mirrored on your Windows 2000 Server to protect the boot and system volumes. Disk Management reports the mirror volume's status as Failed Redundancy and the disk's status as Offline. You identify and replace the faulty disk with a new dynamic disk, but the Add Mirror command remains unavailable. Why?**
    a. The new disk contains insufficient free disk space.
    b. The new disk should be basic, not dynamic.
    c. An incorrect file system appears on the new disk.
    d. You should use the Reactivate Disk command.
2. **You were recently called to a remote customer site to investigate why data on a striped set with parity can be accessed only slowly. You discover that the volume status is Failed Redundancy, so you immediately try to repair the RAID 5 array by running the Repair Volume Command. This effort fails to return the array to Healthy status. Which command can you execute to rebuild the fault tolerant array?**
    a. Reactivate Disk
    b. Regenerate Parity
    c. Reactivate Volume
    d. Repair Disk
3. **You have a Windows 2000 Server configured with two hard disks, disk 0 and disk 1. The boot and system partitions are located on disk 0 and mirrored on disk 1. When you perform routine maintenance on the server, you notice that disk 1 is showing Failed Redundancy as its disk volume status. How would you remedy this situation?**
    a. Use the Reactivate Disk command.
    b. Use the Repair Volume command.
    c. Use the Add Mirror command.
    d. Use the Repair Mirror command.
4. **Regarding the configuration in Question 3, you attempt to repair the mirror volume by using the Reactivate Disk command, but this effort fails to bring the disk back online. What should you do now to recover the mirror?**
    a. Use the Remove Mirror command to break the mirror, replace the failed disk, and run the Add Mirror command.
    b. Use the Break Mirror command, replace the failed disk, and run the Create New Mirror command.
    c. Format the failed disk with the NTFS, convert it to a basic disk along with the healthy disk, and recreate the mirror.
    d. Replace the failed disk with a disk from another Windows 2000 machine, copy all files from disk 0 to disk 1, and use the Resynchronize Mirror command to rebuild the mirror.

Section 6

Configuring and Troubleshooting Windows 2000 Network Connections

OBJECTIVES

6.1 Install and configure shared access

CONNECTION SHARING • NAT

UNDERSTANDING THE OBJECTIVE

Windows 2000 offers several options for allowing multiple computers to share one link to the Internet, including Connection Sharing and Network Address Translation. Connection Sharing is the simpler of the two to install and configure, but **NAT** offers more configuration options and greater flexibility.

WHAT YOU REALLY NEED TO KNOW

- Connection Sharing is aimed at small networks, whereas NAT is designed for use in medium-sized networks.
- Both Connection Sharing and NAT require two connections: a LAN connection and a connection to the Internet.
- DHCP and DNS are automatically configured (and can't be changed) when Connection Sharing is employed. The "full versions" of these services are not needed, as all necessary functionality is part of the "Internet Connection Sharing" service. All private IP addresses are on the 192.168.0.0/24 network. Autodial may be enabled, if desired.
- NAT requires **RRAS** to be properly installed and configured. Configure it by using the RRAS Setup Wizard or by manually adding NAT as a routing protocol.
- Connection Sharing allows access only to resources on the Connection Sharing computer. NAT allows access to information on computers in the private network (via special ports [port mapping]).
- NAT uses DHCP to assign IP addresses. DHCP must exist and be properly configured on the private network, either on the machine with NAT or any other computer on that network.

OBJECTIVES ON THE JOB

Both Connection Sharing and NAT provide similar capabilities, but take different approaches to get there. Connection Sharing usually applies to home networks, **SOHO** networks, and small offices (those with only a few users). To obtain more control or customizability, you can use NAT. It is typically employed in medium-sized offices where a network administrator is present or readily available. Neither service acts as a firewall or is intended to replace a firewall. If the private network contains sensitive data, consider implementing either a hardware (such as a Cisco PIX) or software (such as Microsoft's ISA Server or Novell's Border Manager) firewall.

PRACTICE TEST QUESTIONS

The network administrator of the Acme Company wants to provide Internet access for seven salespeople who check their e-mail and have Web access at a small branch office. The office currently uses static IP addresses. Only one computer has a modem and phone line, which the salespeople must share to obtain Internet access. All machines in the office run Windows 2000. The home office provides the support and configuration for these machines.

1. **Which of the following configuration changes is necessary to implement NAT? (Choose all that apply.)**
    a. Clients must be configured for DHCP.
    b. A DHCP server must be installed and configured.
    c. A DNS server must be installed and configured.
    d. RRAS must be installed and configured.
    e. A demand-dial interface must be created in RRAS.
    f. Routing must be configured on the dial-up port in RRAS.
    g. The current machine must have the existing connection shared.
    h. A new Internet connection must be created and then shared.
2. **Which of the following configuration changes is necessary to implement Connection Sharing? (Choose all that apply.)**
    a. Clients must be configured for DHCP.
    b. A DHCP server must be installed and configured.
    c. A DNS server must be installed and configured.
    d. RRAS must be installed and configured.
    e. A demand-dial interface must be created in RRAS.
    f. Routing must be configured on the dial-up port in RRAS.
    g. The current machine must have the existing connection shared.
    h. A new Internet connection must be created and then shared.
3. **The network administrator decides that the modem and analog phone line do not provide enough bandwidth and replaces them with a DSL line. Given this new configuration, which of the following changes is necessary to implement NAT? (Choose all that apply.)**
    a. Clients must be configured for DHCP.
    b. A DHCP server must be installed and configured.
    c. A DNS server must be installed and configured.
    d. RRAS must be installed and configured.
    e. A demand-dial interface must be created in RRAS.
    f. Routing must be configured on the dial-up port in RRAS.
    g. The current machine must have the existing connection shared.
    h. A new Internet connection must be created and then shared.

OBJECTIVES

6.2 Troubleshooting shared access

RRAS • INTERNET CONNECTION SHARING • DEMAND DIAL

UNDERSTANDING THE OBJECTIVE

Windows 2000 supports sharing of Internet access among several computers. This shared access can be simple or somewhat complex to provide, with several problems commonly arising. Knowing these common problems and their solutions will allow you to quickly resolve the difficulties.

WHAT YOU REALLY NEED TO KNOW

- Verify that the modem is working properly. If errors arise, then the problem may lie with the modem, the drivers for the modem, the port, the configuration of the port, and so forth.
- Make sure that the Internet Connection service is running if you are using Connection Sharing, or that the Routing and Remote Access Service is running if you are using NAT. Start the service, if necessary. If that effort fails, try to reshare the connection if you are using Connection Sharing, or check the configuration of RRAS if you are using NAT.
- With NAT, verify that IP is enabled on both the LAN and WAN (to the Internet) interfaces and that routing is enabled. Also, confirm that TCP/UDP port translation is enabled.
- With NAT, eliminate any conflicting input or output filters that are blocking Internet traffic.
- Using either method, verify that the clients are configured as DHCP clients with valid IP addresses (typically, 192.168.9.0/24 addresses). If the clients have 169.254.0.0/16 addresses, verify that DHCP is set up correctly.
- If your connection is not always connected to the Internet, check the Enable demand dialing check box if you are using Connection Sharing, or create a demand-dial interface if you are using NAT.

OBJECTIVES ON THE JOB

Businesses increasingly need to provide Internet access to all of their employees. Home users, in turn, often have multiple computers at home and want all of them to share a single connection, especially if it is a high-speed connection. Both Connection Sharing and NAT provide solutions to these problems right out of the box. Problems may arise in these services' configuration, however, and knowing a quick solution to the problem is important in establishing your credibility as a Windows 2000 expert and in fixing the problem in a timely manner.

PRACTICE TEST QUESTIONS

1. **A user can't connect the Connection Sharing machine to the Internet. The name and password are known to be good, as is the modem cable. What should you check next?**
    a. Verify that the ISP's hardware is working correctly.
    b. Verify that the modem is responding properly.
    c. Verify that the Internet Connection Sharing service is enabled.
    d. Verify that a DNS server is configured.
2. **Connection Sharing has been installed and configured on a network. Now all but one computer can connect to the Internet and access resources. What should you check first?**
    a. The IP address on the computer that can't connect
    b. The IP address assigned by the ISP
    c. The status of the Internet Connection Sharing service
    d. The DNS configuration on the client that can't connect
3. **NAT has been installed and configured on a network. Now no one can access the Internet from any computer except for the one that is sharing the Internet connection. What are the two most likely causes of the problem?**
    a. The RRAS service has not been installed.
    b. Clients aren't configured to obtain an IP address automatically.
    c. The RRAS service has not been started.
    d. The Internet Connection Sharing service has not been started.
4. **Connection Sharing has been installed and configured. All clients have IP addresses on the 172.16.0.0/16 network. No one can access the Internet from any computer, except for the one that is sharing the Internet connection. What is the most likely cause of the problem?**
    a. The Internet Connection Sharing service has stopped.
    b. Clients can't find a DHCP server and are using the private IP addressing capabilities of Windows 2000.
    c. Filters on the packets prevent them from reaching other computers.
    d. The clients aren't configured for DHCP.
    e. There is not enough information given to determine the most likely cause of the problem.
5. **You have an ISDN connection to the Internet that you always leave activated. Last night, a power failure caused all of your computers to reboot. Today, several people report that they cannot access the Internet. What is the most likely cause of the problem?**
    a. The Routing and Remote Access service has not been started.
    b. The Internet Connection Sharing service has not been started.
    c. Demand dialing isn't properly configured.
    d. The client computers rebooted before the server was rebooted and didn't recieve valid IP addresses.
    d. There is not enough information given to determine the most likely cause of the problem.

OBJECTIVES

6.3 Install and configure a VPN

VPN • PPTP • L2TP • IPSEC

UNDERSTANDING THE OBJECTIVE

Virtual private networks are created when two or more networks connect to each other securely over a public network (most often the Internet). They save money by allowing each network linked in the **VPN** to connect to a local **ISP** instead of directly to each other. The configuration of a VPN involves the installation and configuration of RRAS, and then implementation of either **PPTP** or **L2TP/IPSec**.

WHAT YOU REALLY NEED TO KNOW

- PPTP is primarily a Microsoft-only standard, although some third parties support it. It includes the ability to set up a tunnel, or virtual path, through an IP-based network between two networks and to encrypt the data that moves through the tunnel.
- L2TP is a protocol for setting up a tunnel between two networks. This proposed **RFC** standard creates the tunnel for the data and supports tunnel authentication, but does not encrypt the data that moves through the tunnel; this task is left for other protocols (typically IPSec).
- Both IP and **IPX** can be tunneled by either PPTP or L2TP.
- IPSec is a protocol for encrypting data through any of several standards, including Data Encryption Standard, Triple **DES**, and 40-bit **BES**.
- IPSec policies can be managed through group policies and remain transparent to users and applications.
- RRAS must be installed and configured to create a VPN. A wizard can help you create a VPN server or a VPN client.
- The calling router (the VPN client) must be configured with an interface plus the correct port type (PPTP or L2TP, depending on how the VPN server is configured—they must be the same); the interface must specify the IP address or host name of the answering router (the VPN server). You must first configure the VPN client's connection to the Internet.
- A user account and password are required on the VPN client, which will be validated by the VPN server. The account must have been granted dial-in permission on the VPN server.

OBJECTIVES ON THE JOB

VPNs are becoming increasingly prevalent in business. Demand for them is currently quite high, but the supply of experts who know how to set up and configure them is limited. VPNs are highly compelling because most businesses already have Internet connections and don't want to pay for redundant connections.

PRACTICE TEST QUESTIONS

1. **What is the primary difference between PPTP and L2TP?**
   a. PPTP provides data encryption; L2TP does not.
   b. L2TP provides data encryption; PPTP does not.
   c. PPTP allows IPX traffic to be tunneled; L2TP does not.
   d. L2TP allows IPX traffic to be tunneled; PPTP does not.
   e. There is no difference between these two protocols.
2. **A VPN server may be configured with Connection Sharing instead of RRAS to simplify the setup of a VPN.**
   a. True
   b. False
3. **You can use IPSec to encrypt IPX traffic as well as IP traffic, thereby creating a secure FVPN when you use IPSec in conjunction with L2TP.**
   a. True
   b. False
4. **You must use IPSec to create a secure VPN.**
   a. True
   b. False
5. **What is the maximum number of VPN ports available on a Windows 2000-based server?**
   a. 1
   b. 10
   c. 256
   d. Virtually unlimited
6. **A VPN client must first ______________ before it can ________________.**
   a. have Connection Sharing installed; have RRAS installed
   b. have L2TP installed; have IPSec installed
   c. connect to the VPN; connect to the Internet
   d. connect to the Internet; connect to the VPN
7. **L2TP provides the ______________, and IPSec provides the ________________.**
   a. logical link; data link
   b. tunnel; encryption
   c. encryption; tunnel
   d. IP-to-MAC translation; name-to-IP translation

OBJECTIVES

6.4 Troubleshoot a VPN

PPTP PORT • L2TP PORT • RAS POLICIES • INPUT AND OUTPUT FILTERS

UNDERSTANDING THE OBJECTIVE

Although VPNs are very powerful and popular, many things can go wrong that will prevent a VPN from working properly. To ensure that network communication proceeds as planned, you should recognize common problems relating to VPNs and know how to resolve them.

WHAT YOU REALLY NEED TO KNOW

- A VPN connection cannot be created if RRAS isn't installed and properly configured on the VPN server or if RRAS is stopped.
- Both the client and server must use the same type of port (L2TP or PPTP). Windows 2000 supports both port types, whereas pre-Windows 2000 operating systems support only PPTP.
- A port of the correct type is required to complete a VPN connection; if none is available, the connection will be refused.
- The same LAN protocol must exist on both LANs (inside the two VPNs) and be enabled on the RRAS server.
- You should verify that the RAS policy settings are compatible on both sides, including settings related to authentication and encryption.
- You should verify that enough IP addresses are available in the static IP address pool (if it is used). If an IPX client requests its own IPX mode number, confirm that the server allows clients to request their own mode numbers. IPX network numbers must be unique to the network.
- If some traffic gets through the connection, but other traffic is blocked, verify that the appropriate input and output filters are in place. For example, by default, ICMP traffic associated with use of the PING utility is discarded.

OBJECTIVES ON THE JOB

Many people remain somewhat wary of placing company information on the Internet, even when the data is encrypted. For this reason (and to maintain the availability of connectivity), VPNs must be set up and running with minimal problems and delay, but adequate security. Knowing the solutions needed to complete these tasks will help you meet this goal.

PRACTICE TEST QUESTIONS

1. **A Windows NT 4.0 VPN client attempts to connect to a Windows 2000 VPN server, but its effort fails. What is the most likely reason?**
   a. Windows NT 4.0 doesn't support L2TP.
   b. Windows NT 4.0 doesn't support PPTP.
   c. Windows 2000 VPN servers support only Windows 2000 VPN clients.
   d. IPSec is configured incorrectly on the VPN client.
2. **A VPN has been set up and worked in the past. Since the company changed ISPs, however, it has not worked correctly. What are the two most likely reasons?**
   a. The RRAS service is stopped.
   b. The Internet Connection Sharing service is stopped.
   c. The new ISP is providing a different IP address to the demand-dial interface.
   d. The VPN connection is autodialing the original ISP connection, rather than the new connection.
3. **Your company has grown from 5 sites to 12. As it has grown, more VPNs have been configured. Now some sites can connect only intermittently. What is the most likely cause of the problem?**
   a. Windows 2000 supports only 10 simultaneous VPN connections.
   b. Not enough PPTP or L2TP ports are available.
   c. RRAS isn't configured properly at some sites.
   d. Different sites have different IPSec settings.
4. **A site that includes only NetWare clients and servers wants to access resources at other sites. Windows 2000 Server has been installed and configured to provide the necessary VPN services. Although RRAS has been set up correctly and Internet resources can be accessed from the VPN server, clients can't access resources in other sites. What should you check first?**
   a. SAP is configured incorrectly.
   b. Connection Sharing must be configured first.
   c. IPX is properly configured in the other sites.
   d. NetWare clients and servers can't use VPNs.
5. **Widgets, Inc., wants to connect two sites with a VPN. Although both sites have Internet access and users at both sites can access Internet resources without any problems, the two sites can't connect to each other. Which of the following reasons might be causing this problem? (Choose all that apply.)**
   a. The static IP address pool is too small.
   b. The two LANs use different protocols.
   c. The Routing and Remote Access Service is stopped.
   d. A VPN connection has not been created between the VPN client and the VPN server.
   e. The two sites use different encryption standards.

OBJECTIVES

6.5 Install and configure network protocols

NETWORK PROTOCOLS • INSTALL • CONFIGURE

UNDERSTANDING THE OBJECTIVE

Two primary routable protocols are used in a Windows 2000 network: TCP/IP, which is installed by default, and **NWLink**, which is used with Novell networks. Other protocols are less popular because they do not route (**DLC** and **NetBEUI**) or are a "talkative" protocols when used with Macs. Plug and Play is now a part of Windows 2000; when it detects a network card, it installs the default—the TCP/IP protocol—plus Client Services for Microsoft Networks and File and Print Sharing for Microsoft Networks. TCP/IP is set to obtain an address from a DHCP server.

WHAT YOU REALLY NEED TO KNOW

- TCP/IP is the only protocol bound by default when Windows 2000 detects the NIC.
- Windows 2000 supports five network protocols: TCP/IP, NWLink, AppleTalk, DLC, and NetBEUI. **ATM**, **IrDA**, and others are also available.
- In addition to the TCP/IP protocol, Client Services for Microsoft Networks and File and Print Sharing for Microsoft Networks are installed upon detection.
- By default, a Windows 2000 Professional machine expects to receive its IP addresses dynamically from a DHCP server.
- A valid IP address and subnet mask are required for a LAN.
- A default gateway is also required if you plan to connect more than one LAN or use the Internet.
- When installed, NWLink automatically detects the frame type. If two frame types are present, you must manually configure each client to be able to access both.
- When installing Gateway Services for Netware, Client Services for Netware and NWLink are automatically installed.
- Only TCP/IP is supported for access to Active Directory services.
- The first octet of a Class A address has a range of 1–126 (127 is reserved for the loopback address), a Class B address has range of 128–191, and a Class C address has a range of 192–223.

OBJECTIVES ON THE JOB

With Windows 2000, the network administrator's job has been simplified with regard to the installation and configuration of the network protocols. Plug and Play detects cards and performs a standard TCP/IP installation. Windows 2000 can also take advantage of Automatic Private Addressing for your clients. No routing is available with this option nor can clients access DNS servers.

PRACTICE TEST QUESTIONS

1. **You found a second NIC in your office and want to install it in one of your Web servers. When you install it, Plug and Play does not detect it. What must you do to install this network card?**
    a. Reboot the server.
    b. Place the NIC in another slot.
    c. Manually configure the card using the Make New Connection Wizard in Network Neighborhood.
    d. Use the Add/Remove Hardware wizard in the Control Panel.
2. **The following protocols are installed on all of your client computers, in the following order: NWLink, TCP/IP, and NetBEUI. Some users complain that connecting to a Windows 2000 server takes too long. How can you speed up the connection to the Windows 2000 servers?**
    a. Place TCP/IP at the top of the binding order on the client.
    b. Place TCP/IP at the top of the binding order on the server.
    c. Place NetBEUI at the top of the binding order on the client.
    d. Place NetBEUI at the top of the binding order on the server.
3. **What is the class and default subnet mask for the address 220.200.54.78?**
    a. Class A, 255.0.0.0
    b. Class B, 255.255.0.0
    c. Class C, 255.255.255.0
    d. Class D, 255.255.255.255
4. **If a single NetWare server exists on your network, when you install CSNW on a client, you must adjust the frame type.**
    a. True
    b. False
5. **If you have more than one NetWare server running 802.3 and 802.0 frame types and need to connect to each server, what settings must be established for the frame type?**
    a. None, leave as auto
    b. Ethernet II
    c. Manually configure for both frame types
    d. Manually configure a single frame type, as you can connect using only one frame type at a time
6. **Which two computers are on the same subnet?**
    a. 60.35 40.9 and 60.68. 4010, subnet mask of 255.244.0.0
    b. 60.35 40.9 and 60.68. 4010, subnet mask of 255.240.0.0
    c. 60.35.40.9 and 60.35. 60.10, subnet mask of 255.224.0.0
    c. 60.35. 40.9 and 60.35. 60.10, subnet mask of 255.240.0.0

OBJECTIVES

6.6 Troubleshoot network protocols

IPCONFIG • PING • TROUBLESHOOTING

UNDERSTANDING THE OBJECTIVE

The protocols and the tools to troubleshoot them have not changed dramatically with the introduction of Windows 2000. A feature that is available in Windows 2000 but was not available in Windows NT, is Automatic Private Addressing. PING and IPCONFIG continue to be very useful tools in determining connectivity. Frame type mismatches are common mistakes in NetWare connectivity, whereas incorrect subnet masks are common errors in TCP/IP connectivity.

WHAT YOU REALLY NEED TO KNOW

- An address from the 169.254.0.0 network and a subnet mask of 255.255.0.0 indicate that an address was not obtained from DHCP but is using an Automatic Private Address. Additionally, no DNS service is reachable.
- You should know how to use the following utilities: PING, ARP, IPCONFIG, NBTSTAT, NETSTAT, ROUTE, HOSTNAME, and TRACERT. PING and IPCONFIG are the most common and will likely be covered on the exam.
- You can disable Automatic IP Addressing through the Registry.
- Use **CSNW** on all clients connecting to NetWare servers or use **GSNW** with Windows 2000 servers, but not both.
- Bind the most often-used protocols at the top of the order on each client.
- Enable NetBIOS to see network computers in a mixed client environment, such as Windows 98 or NT.
- You should know your default and custom subnet masks and be able to determine which network your machine uses.
- You should know where DHCP and relay agents need to be placed for connectivity.

OBJECTIVES ON THE JOB

If you have difficulty reaching the Windows 2000 domain, first check your NIC's connectivity by pinging the loopback address (127.0/0/1) and viewing the IPCONFIG information. Check other connectivity by pinging internal network addresses, the default gateway, and external addresses. Addresses in the 169.254.0.0 range may indicate that your DHCP server is not providing IP addresses.

PRACTICE TEST QUESTIONS

You have the following network: Subnet A has 140 Windows 2000 Professional machines and 25 Windows NT machines, all running TCP/IP with the IP addresses obtained dynamically. The network includes four Windows 2000 Servers, one of which acts as a DHCP server and a primary DNS zone. The scope of addresses is 204.133.50.11–204.133.50.2000, with a subnet mask of 255.255.255.192. All servers use static addresses in the range 204.133.50.1–204.133.50.4, and the default gateway is 204.133.50.1.

1. **Some of the users on Subnet A complain that they cannot log on to your network and do not have Internet access. What is required to solve this problem? (Select two.)**
   a. Install a WINS server on each subnet.
   b. Change the server using 204.133.50.1 to 204.133.50.5.
   c. Change the subnet mask on Subnet A to 255.255.255.224.
   d. Change the subnet mask on Subnet A to 255.255.255.0.
2. **None of the client machines on your network can connect to resources on the network. You realize that the WINS tab on the Advanced TCP/IP settings is improperly configured. LMHOSTS files will not be used. What selections should be made to allow clients to connect?**
   a. LMHOSTS check box not selected and Enable NetBIOS over TCP/IP
   b. LMHOSTS check box not selected and Disable NetBIOS over TCP/IP
   c. LMHOSTS check box selected and Enable NetBIOS over TCP/IP
   d. LMHOSTS check box selected and Disable NetBIOS over TCP/IP
3. **You install a Novell NetWare 4.x print server on your network. You manually set the frame type on each client to 802.3. You are unable to connect to the Novell server. Which setting allows clients to connect using CSNW and NWLink? (Choose all that apply.)**
   a. Frame Type of 802.2
   b. Frame Type set to Auto
   c. Frame Type set to Ethernet II
   d. Frame Type set to 802.5
4. **After installing the NetWare server, instead of client software, which components would need to be installed on Windows 2000 Server to allow clients access? (Choose all that apply.)**
   a. File and Print Sharing for NetWare
   b. GSNW
   c. NWLink NetBIOS
   d. IPX/SPX/NetBIOS Compatible Transport Protocol

OBJECTIVES

6.7 Install and configure network services

WINS • DHCP • INSTALL • CONFIGURE

UNDERSTANDING THE OBJECTIVE

Windows 2000 can eliminate the need for a WINS server in a pure Windows 2000 environment using Dynamic DNS; it does, however, support WINS in a mixed environment and during migrations. When possible, the Administrator should take advantage of the DHCP service as well as Active Directory Integrated DNS zones. In Windows 2000, the DHCP server must be authorized in Active Directory to allow its use.

WHAT YOU REALLY NEED TO KNOW

- The four steps of the DHCP lease process are DHCPDISCOVER, DHCPOFFER, DHCPREQUEST, and DHCPACK, in that order.
- Requirements for a DHCP server include: a static IP address, a subnet mask, the DHCP service, a range of addresses, and authorization from the Active Directory services.
- You may configure options for the server, the scope, or the client.
- Common options include the default gateway (Router 003), the DNS servers (006), WINS options, and needing both (044) for the IP address and (046) for the Mode type.
- DHCP client lease renewals occur at 50% of the renewal time. If no server is available, then a broadcast is made to any DHCP server on the network at 87.5% of the renewal time.
- To utilize DHCP in a routed environment, you must have one of the following in place: an RFC1542-compliant router, a DHCP server on each subnet, or a DHCP relay agent on subnets that do not contain a DCHP server.
- WINS proxies are used for non-WINS clients, such as UNIX machines.
- WINS servers are not required on every subnet.
- Three types of DNS zones exist: standard primary, standard secondary, and Active Directory integrated.

OBJECTIVES ON THE JOB

In native mode with all Windows 2000 clients, you can use DHCP along with Active Directory integrated zones on more than one computer to provide redundancy and name registration on every machine on your network. All domain controllers synchronize DNS information with one another to provide your network with reliable name resolution. In mixed mode, you should use WINS in conjunction with DHCP, a standard primary DNS zone, and at least one standard secondary DNS zone to provide both name resolution and redundancy.

PRACTICE TEST QUESTIONS

You have the following network: Subnet A has 140 Windows 2000 Professional machines running TCP/IP, with the IP addresses obtained dynamically. The network includes four Windows 2000 Servers, one of which acts as a DHCP server and a primary DNS zone. The scope of addresses is 204.133.50.11–204.133.50.2000, with a subnet mask of 255.255.255.192. All servers use static addresses in the range 204.133.50.1–204.133.50.4, and the default gateway is 204.133.50.1.

Subnet B has 50 Windows NT machines running TCP/IP, with the IP addresses obtained dynamically. The network includes two Windows 2000 Servers, one of which runs DHCP. The scope of addresses is 204.133.51.11–204.133.51.1000, with a subnet mask of 255.255.255.255.0. The IP addresses of the servers are 204.133.51.2 and 204.133.51.3, and the default gateway is 204.133.51.1.

1. **Users on Subnet A can access the Internet. Subnet B users can access sites only via their IP addresses. How can you resolve this problem with the least amount of administrative effort?**
    a. Change the DNS scope option for the DHCP server on Subnet B.
    b. Install a secondary DNS server on Subnet A.
    c. Change the DNS configuration manually on each client in Subnet B.
    d. Install a secondary DNS server on Subnet B.
2. **A user tries to use a NET USE command to connect to a share on a server and fails, yet the user can use FTP to access that share. What should you do to allow this user to employ this command? (Choose all that apply.)**
    a. Make the user a member of the Administrators group.
    b. Install an Active Directory integrated DNS server.
    c. Install a WINS proxy on Subnet A.
    d. Install a WINS proxy on Subnet B.
    e. Configure all DHCP scope options to point to a WINS server.

OBJECTIVES

6.8 Configure remote access

RRAS • REMOTE ACCESS

UNDERSTANDING THE OBJECTIVE

Windows 2000 provides two methods of supporting remote access: **RAS** or a VPN. RAS involves a direct connection to the server via a modem, an **ISDN** adapter, or nullmodem cable. Knowledge of remote access policies is critical on the server exam. Unlike with Windows NT, RRAS is installed by default with Windows 2000 but leaves it in a disabled state until you configure it through the RRAS snap-in.

WHAT YOU REALLY NEED TO KNOW

- RRAS is installed with Windows 2000 but is disabled; accessing the snap-in for the first time enables it.
- The two types of authentication providers are Windows authentication and **RADIUS** authentication.
- RADIUS authentication is a good solution with multiple RAS servers.
- A RAS server can act as an Internet Connection server, VPN server, or router.
- The protocols applied by default to the RAS server are those installed on your server. You may add others if necessary.
- If the top protocol bound to your connection does not match the top protocol on the client, the client may get an error but eventually connects when a protocol match occurs.
- If the authentication methods or encryption methods do not match, connections cannot be made.
- Callback options consist of No Callback, Callback Set by Caller, and Always Callback to: _______.

OBJECTIVES ON THE JOB

Windows 2000 RAS connections allow for more granular control. If you have a user account in a Windows NT domain or in Windows 2000 mixed mode, you have only the option to Allow or Deny Access. In contrast, Windows 2000 allows you to define conditions based on groups or users, define times for accounts to access the server, configure different authentication methods, and utilize the RADIUS server.

PRACTICE TEST QUESTIONS

1. **To install a RAS server, what must you do?**
    a. Start the Routing and Remote Access utility through the Add/Remove Programs applet.
    b. Start the Routing and Remote Access utility through the Computer Management snap-in.
    c. Start the Routing and Remote Access utility through the Administrative Tools menu.
    d. Install RRAS from the Windows 2000 Resource Kit.
2. **Which is not an option when configuring a RRAS server?**
    a. Internet Connection Sharing Server
    b. Internet Connection Server
    c. VPN Server
    d. Router
3. **A RAS server can be configured for "outbound connections only" through the port properties sheet.**
    a. True
    b. False
4. **Which of the following acts as an authentication provider? (Choose all that apply.)**
    a. Windows 2000 member server
    b. Windows 2000 domain controller
    c. Windows NT member server
    d. Windows NT PDC
    e. A RADIUS server
5. **Which clients may connect to a Windows 2000 RAS server? (Choose all that apply.)**
    a. Windows 3.1
    b. Windows for Workgroups
    c. Windows NT 3.51
    d. Windows 95
6. **Windows 2000 supports SLIP dial-up connections.**
    a. True
    b. False
7. **What is the default policy that applies after installing the RRAS server?**
    a. Everyone group, Full Access anytime
    b. Administrators group, Full Access anytime
    c. Anyone attempting to access, Denied Access
    d. The default policy as defined during setup through the RRAS Wizard

OBJECTIVES

6.9 Monitor remote access

RRAS • REMOTE ACCESS

UNDERSTANDING THE OBJECTIVE

Routing and Remote Access Services in Windows 2000 is much more sophisticated than that found in Windows NT 4.0. In addition to controlling access through policies, you can monitor the users, ports, and problems associated with RRAS in an easy and efficient way. Through the RRAS snap-in, you may view current users and ports. You can also configure logging of PPP events to the Event Log if desired as well as differing degrees of monitoring.

WHAT YOU REALLY NEED TO KNOW

- Bandwidth can be controlled on multilink connections via a protocol new to Windows 2000, **BAP**.
- You may monitor how many and which users are connected through the RRAS snap-in.
- You can configure RRAS in several ways to write events to the System Event Log.
- You can configure RRAS to write **PPP** events to a log file in the \\windir\tracing folder.
- You can determine which ports are active through the RRAS snap-in.
- Under Dial-in Constraints, you can disconnect a user if that user is idle for a predetermined amount of time.
- Under Dial-in Constraints, you can restrict the maximum session length, the days of the week on which dial-ins are permitted, and the time of day during which dial-ins are permitted.
- The combination of several physical connections into one logical connection known as multilinking is supported and can be controlled in an RRAS policy.

OBJECTIVES ON THE JOB

RRAS in Windows 2000 is far superior than that found in Windows NT 4.0. You can set up policies and then, based on those policies, create profiles for particular times, user groups, and so on. After creating these policies, you can monitor active users or ports to identify unauthorized users or trouble spots in either your policy or hardware configurations. With the active users option, you can determine how long those users have been logged on, count packets in and out, calculate a compression ratio, find a network address, and even disconnect the user. You can have RRAS events written to the System Log based on errors only, for warning, or for maximum information; you can also decline logging.

PRACTICE TEST QUESTIONS

1. **You are concerned about using your network bandwidth effectively when users dial in via the multilink capabilities. Which new feature in Windows 2000 allows for achieving this efficiency?**
   a. MultiLink Bandwidth Throttling
   b. Bandwidth Allocation Protocol
   c. Bandwidth Throttling Protocol
   d. Can be done only with single-line dial-in users
2. **Which information is available to administrators from the RRAS snap-in to monitor users? (Choose all that apply.)**
   a. How many users are connected
   b. Which users are connected
   c. Which computers are connected
   d. Which groups have members connected
3. **It is possible to determine which ports are active from the RRAS snap-in.**
   a. True
   b. False
4. **What is an effective method to prevent unauthorized users from randomly guessing user names and passwords to gain access to your RAS server? (Choose all that apply.)**
   a. Use the Remote Account Lockout feature on the RAS server.
   b. Use the Account Lockout feature from the Dial-in properties of each user.
   c. Utilize the CallerID feature.
   d. Utilize the Callback feature to a specific number.
5. **Event logging and PPP logging can be enabled simultaneously.**
   a. True
   b. False
6. **Event logging writes to the Event Log; where is PPP logging written?**
   a. Application Log
   b. \\windir\tracing\ppp.log
   c. \\windir\system32\ppp.log
   d. \\windir\system32\RAS\ppp.log
7. **Some of your users deal with sensitive data; and their settings should be more restrictive than those of the other users. What is the best way to accomplish this goal?**
   a. Create and configure an OU for these users and grant the Allow Remote Access permission to that OU.
   b. Create a separate RAS policy on the RAS server and include those members in the policy.
   c. Create and configure an OU for the RAS server(s) and allow the restrictive groups to access the server.
   d. All users must use the same security settings.

OBJECTIVES

6.10 Troubleshoot remote access

RRAS • REMOTE ACCESS • PPP LOGGING

UNDERSTANDING THE OBJECTIVE

Windows 2000 includes several tools to aid in troubleshooting, such as tracing, event logging, and PPP logging. Tracing can record function calls and interactions while performing file tracing, which is enabled in the Registry. Logging of events can be set for no logging, errors only, and errors and warnings to the maximum information available. PPP logging can be enabled and writes to a log file in the \\windir\tracing directory.

WHAT YOU REALLY NEED TO KNOW

- Protocols must match on both the client and the server to establish a connection.
- Authentication and encryption methods must also match to establish a connection.
- Event logging writes to the System Log file. You can set the level from no logging to maximum logging.
- Access policies are set through the remote access policies, rather than through the domain or group policy.
- You may view active ports and users through the RRAS snap-in.
- Session time and inactivity time settings can log off users when you define them in the profile of a remote access policy.
- The default profile allows no one access at any time; that profile must be edited or new profiles created to allow access.
- You should know how remote access policies are applied.

OBJECTIVES ON THE JOB

Windows 2000 RRAS offers enhanced troubleshooting tools to administrators through the RRAS snap-in. Administrators can easily set up RAS event and PPP logging, view active users or ports, and set up tracing for complex network issues. You should know the encryption and authentication methods for your server and the configurations of the clients. Administrators should also understand how remote access policies are configured and applied.

PRACTICE TEST QUESTIONS

Your department supports more than 1000 remote users. You have several Windows 2000 RAS servers that use a RADIUS server to authenticate your remote users, with the authentication method being set to MS-CHAP v2. Twenty-five modems are connected to these servers. Users can dial in with the NetBEUI and TCP/IP protocols, which are bound in that order.

1. **You want to define the access policies for one of the RAS servers. You open the RRAS snap-in but do not see the Remote Access Policies option. How can you access this policy option?**
   a. Add the option for Remote Access Policies snap-in from the Action menu.
   b. Access the Remote Access Policies through the Users and Computers in Active Directory.
   c. Access policies through the RADIUS authentication provider interface.
   d. Run the Routing and Remote Access Server Wizard.
2. **Occasionally, your users complain that they have trouble connecting to the server. After they try two or three times, they can connect. The problem never affects more than one user at a time. What should you investigate first?**
   a. The RAS policy on each server
   b. The RAS policy on the RADIUS server
   c. The Device Manager and each modem's properties
   d. Dial-in properties of the user affected in Active Directory
3. **Since you installed the RAS servers, almost all of the users complain about receiving an error message before connecting to the server. What might cause this problem?**
   a. NetBEUI is not installed on the client.
   b. NetBEUI is not installed on the server.
   c. NetBEUI is bound first on the client.
   d. NetBEUI is bound last on the server.
4. **Some of the users are denied access whenever they attempt to connect. What should you check as the most probable cause of the problem?**
   a. Authentication method on the server
   b. Authentication method on the client
   c. Protocols installed on the clients
   d. Operating system of the clients
5. **Occasionally, users connect but are then dropped. What is the best way for an administrator to look for problems that may be affecting large groups of users?**
   a. Enable RAS logging and view the Application Log.
   b. Enable RAS logging and view the System Log.
   c. Enable Event logging and view the Application Log.
   d. Enable Event logging and view the System Log.

OBJECTIVES

6.11 Create and configure a remote access policy and profile

RRAS • REMOTE ACCESS POLICY • REMOTE ACCESS PROFILE

UNDERSTANDING THE OBJECTIVE

A remote access policy is a profile that is applied to a given set of conditions. You create a policy by first selecting a condition that must be met, such as group membership or time restrictions. After defining the condition, you must edit the profile that will be applied when the condition arises. Options available for the profile include dial-in constraints, IP address assignment policy, multilink settings, authentication methods, encryption settings, and advanced connection attributes.

WHAT YOU REALLY NEED TO KNOW

- Remote access policies control access; the group policy does not.
- Access policies reside on either the RAS server or the RADIUS server (if a RADIUS server is the authentication provider).
- When the network uses a RADIUS server, the remote access policy mode is not available on the RAS server and must be accessed on the RADIUS server.
- Policies are applied in order and can be changed. The first policy for which matching criteria are found is applied.
- The default authentication protocols are **MS-CHAP** and MS-CHAPv2.
- Deny Access to Everyone is the default policy.
- Clients and the server must agree on encryption methods so as to connect to each other.
- VPNs support PPTP and L2TP.
- The most common policy is based on Windows group membership.

OBJECTIVES ON THE JOB

You must set up a policy or multiple policies to manage access to your RAS servers. By default, the following condition is enabled: all hours of the day, every day of the week, Deny Access. You can set conditions such as time restrictions, group memberships, caller ID, protocol type, tunnel type, and others. Additional settings within the profile of the condition can restrict logon time, bandwidth allocation, encryption, and authentication methods.

PRACTICE TEST QUESTIONS

1. **You cannot find the mode for creating remote access policies on your RAS server. How can you access the remote access policy mode?**
   a. Reinstall RRAS.
   b. Install the Remote Access Policy snap-in.
   c. Open the RRAS snap-in on the RADIUS server.
   d. Access the remote access policy in Active Directory.
   e. Log on as the RAS Administrator.
2. **Which of the following is not an option in the Dial-In Constraints tab of each profile?**
   a. Disconnect if idle for...
   b. Restrict maximum session time
   c. Restrict access to the following days and times
   d. Log in from this workstation only
3. **Your user accounts are included in two different remote access policies. How are the policies applied?**
   a. The first policy to match is applied.
   b. The most restrictive policy is applied.
   c. The least restrictive policy is applied.
   d. Cumulative permissions are applied.
4. **What are the default authentication protocols for a RAS server? (Select two.)**
   a. CHAP
   b. MS-CHAP
   c. MS-CHAPv2
   d. EAP
5. **If you configure the server to require data encryption and the client is not configured to perform encryption, how is data transmitted?**
   a. In clear text
   b. You connect and are prompted to select an encrypting protocol
   c. No data is transmitted and the connection is terminated
   d. The server uses public key encryption
6. **VPN support is enabled through a remote access policy that utilizes which protocols? (Choose all that apply.)**
   a. SLIP
   b. PPP
   c. PPTP
   d. L2TP

OBJECTIVES

6.12 Install and configure Terminal Services

TERMINAL SERVICES INSTALLATION AND CONFIGURATION

UNDERSTANDING THE OBJECTIVE

Terminal Services is used to grant thin clients access to shared Windows 2000 resources and applications and to provide remote administration. It requires significant system resources—especially memory—so you should deploy this service with caution.

WHAT YOU REALLY NEED TO KNOW

- Terminal Services can be installed on Windows 2000 Server systems during the initial installation or through the Windows Components area of Add/Remove Programs.
- Terminal Services has two operational modes. Application server mode is used to share applications and resources with thin clients during terminal sessions. Remote administration mode is used to remotely administer servers; it does not support multisession application access.
- When configuring Terminal Services for application server mode, you must decide whether to use security permissions that are compatible with only Windows 2000 or with the widest range of legacy applications.
- You configure Terminal Services through the Terminal Services Configuration Manager.
- Each Windows 2000 user account can be configured to grant or deny Terminal Services connections.

OBJECTIVES ON THE JOB

In most cases, when you are employing Terminal Services as an application server, you should deploy a Windows 2000 Server system for exclusive use by Terminal Services. Each connected user session requires 3 to 9 MB of additional physical RAM. Microsoft recommends that the base system include at least 128 MB of RAM before RAM is added to support connected sessions.

PRACTICE TEST QUESTIONS

1. **DLOP, Inc. has a Windows 2000 network consisting of 15 servers and 460 clients. A new database program is required for some government contract work, but it must be accessed directly on the system where it is installed. The IT budget is nearly depleted. Which of the following is the most cost-effective and realistic solution to ensure that the 20 users who must have access to the database program have the ability can do their work?**
    a. Purchase additional copies of the database program and install them on the clients where needed.
    b. Allow users to log on to the Windows 2000 Server where the database is installed, but limit each user's session to one hour to allow all 20 users to have an access window each day.
    c. Deploy Terminal Services on the Windows 2000 Server where the database will be installed.
    d. No cost-effective solutions are possible in this situation.
2. **Once deployed, users complain that their connection sessions operate extremely slowly. Often, they have to wait 30 seconds or more for their mouse or keyboard actions to show a result on the screen. Which of the following is most likely the culprit?**
    a. Too little RAM on the Terminal Server host computer
    b. Inactivity timeout set too high
    c. Maximum number of simultaneous sessions per adapter has been reached
    d. Terminal Services is installed in remote administration mode
3. **Terminal Services allows computer systems with lower hardware abilities, less RAM, and even older operating systems to exploit the power of Windows 2000 and Windows 2000-compatible applications.**
    a. True
    b. False
4. **Which of the following statements is true?**
    a. Terminal Services must be removed and then reinstalled to alter the mode.
    b. Terminal Services can be installed through the Windows Component area of Add/Remove Programs.
    c. When Terminal Services is installed in remote administration mode, you must select which level or permissions it will use.
    d. Both modes of Terminal Services allow you to access multisession-capable applications.
5. **Which of the following is a possible configuration setting through the Terminal Services Configuration Manager? (Choose all that apply.)**
    a. Enable Clipboard mapping
    b. Session encryption
    c. Remap network drives upon session start
    d. Launch a batch file upon session start
    e. Restrict the number of connections on each NIC

OBJECTIVES

6.13 Monitor Terminal Services

TERMINAL SERVICES MONITORING

UNDERSTANDING THE OBJECTIVE

Terminal Services is monitored through its own utility as well as through several native tools of Windows 2000.

WHAT YOU REALLY NEED TO KNOW

- The Terminal Services Manager offers some insight into the current activities of Terminal Services. You can use this tool to view the status of current client sessions.
- The Terminal Services Manager displays statistics about Terminal Services, including number of active sessions, users, servers, and session processes.
- From this tool you can take over control of a session, oversee the activity in a session, terminate an active session, terminate a process within an active session, send messages to users in client sessions, and restart/reset protocols and connections.
- You can also use the System Monitor to view activities related to Terminal Services.
- Task Manager expands its capabilities to display two additional metric columns on its Processes tab related to Terminal Services and offers the ability to terminate a process across all sessions.
- Terminal Services can be managed and monitored from the command line using the following commands: change logon, change user, change port, cprofile, dbgtrace, flattemp, logoff, msg, query process, query session, query user, register, reset session, shadow, tscon, tsdiscon, tskill, tsprof, and tsshutdn.

OBJECTIVES ON THE JOB

Other than peeking in on the activity of active sessions and monitoring for problems, you rarely need to keep an active watch over Terminal Services. It functions nicely on its own as long as it is properly configured and adequately powered—specifically, when it is given enough physical RAM. For more details on using the command line to manage Terminal Services, see the Windows 2000 Server Resource Kit.

PRACTICE TEST QUESTIONS

1. **Which of the following is an action that can be taken through the Terminal Services Manager? (Choose all that apply.)**
    a. Grant a user account access to Terminal Services
    b. Take over control of a session
    c. Set user permission requirements regarding remote session control
    d. Oversee the activity in a session
    e. Set a simultaneous connected sessions limit for each adapter
    f. Terminate an active session
    g. Terminate a process within an active session
    h. Allow individual logons or force all connections through a single user account
    i. Send messages to users in client sessions
    j. Set an active session time limit, set an idle disconnect limit, and end terminated or disconnected sessions
    k. Restart/reset protocols and connections
    l. Launch programs or batch files on session start
2. **Where can you obtain information about the current activity of Terminal Services easily and directly? (Choose all that apply.)**
    a. System Monitor
    b. Network Monitor
    c. Task Manager
    d. Command prompt
    e. Routing and Remote Access utility
    f. Terminal Services Manager
3. **It is possible both to view the current activity within a Terminal Services session and to take control of the activities within a session.**
    a. True
    b. False
4. **Which of the following statements is true? (Choose all that apply.)**
    a. A process can be terminated for a single session or for all sessions.
    b. Remote control over a session can be configured so that user permission must be granted.
    c. A system administrator can send messages to users while in an active Terminal Services session.
    d. Some aspects of Terminal Services can be managed from batch files.

OBJECTIVES

6.14 Troubleshoot Terminal Services

TERMINAL SERVICES TROUBLESHOOTING

UNDERSTANDING THE OBJECTIVE

Terminal Services is fairly self-supportive, but it is also a complex system. As with most complex systems, problems can occur in many areas. Most, however, are related to communications, permissions, and configurations.

WHAT YOU REALLY NEED TO KNOW

- You can check security permissions related to Terminal Services access, domain access, and resource access.
- If you are attempting to install a new application from an .msi file (that is, through Add/Remove programs) within a Terminal Services session, you must be logged in as an administrator.
- The Terminal Services client for Windows NT will not process an automatic logon correctly, so you must manually log in when using Windows NT as a client.
- Most applications that are installed before the installation of Terminal Services will not function properly. In most cases, you should install applications after Terminal Services is installed. If the application is already present when Terminal Services is installed, remove it and then reinstall it.
- After Terminal Services is removed from a system, most applications will not function properly. They must be removed and then reinstalled.
- Terminal Services and Offline Files cannot function at the same time. They are mutually exclusive services.
- If a session is not functioning properly, manually disconnect (that is, terminate) the session, and then attempt to complete the session connection again.
- If a specific link or a specific network interface continuously hosts problematic sessions, reset the link or update/replace the associated driver.
- Check for reliable network communications.
- Make sure that the Terminal Services system has plenty of physical RAM.
- If only a single client is experiencing or causing problems, remove and reinstall that Terminal Services client.

OBJECTIVES ON THE JOB

Troubleshooting Terminal Services is no different than troubleshooting any other Windows 2000 service. Always test for physical problems first, then proceed from general issues (such as network communications or operating system functionality) to specific issues (such as permissions or configuration settings).

PRACTICE TEST QUESTIONS

1. **FLOP Corporation operates a large network. Some users are assigned to work from thin clients. These clients connect to a Windows 2000 Server hosting Terminal Services so as to access shared applications. One client (out of the 35 that regularly connect to Terminal Services) is experiencing problems. Each time a session connection is attempted for this client, it fails. Likewise, executing a ping command between the client and the Terminal Services server results in no response. Which of the following is most likely the cause of these session connection failures?**
   a. The Terminal Services server does not have enough physical RAM.
   b. The Terminal Services client is a Windows NT system that is attempting an automatic logon.
   c. The Terminal Services server has reached its maximum concurrent sessions limit.
   d. The Terminal Services client has a bad network adapter driver.
2. **After you correct the problem discovered in Question 1, the same client attempts to connect to the Terminal Services server. This time a connection is made, but all activities within the session are sluggish and take several seconds to recognize mouse movements or keyboard strokes. What is the most likely cause of this problem?**
   a. The Terminal Services server does not have enough physical RAM.
   b. The Terminal Services client has "full logging of session" enabled.
   c. The Terminal Services server has reached its maximum concurrent sessions limit.
   d. The Terminal Services client is using high encryption and the Terminal Services server is using low encryption.
3. **When you remove Terminal Services from a system, no other actions are specifically required before the resultant system can be used normally.**
   a. True
   b. False
4. **Which of the following statements is true? (Choose all that apply.)**
   a. Without reliable network communications, Terminal Server sessions will not behave properly.
   b. If you are attempting to install a new application from an .msi file (that is, through Add/Remove Programs) within a Terminal Services session, you must be logged in as an administrator.
   c. The Terminal Services client for Windows 98 will not process an automatic logon correctly, so you must manually log in when using Windows 98 as a client.
   d. Terminal Services and Offline Files cannot function at the same time. They are mutually exclusive services.
   e. When attempted session connections fail, the best first step is to remove and then reinstall Terminal Services.
   f. A single Terminal Services client can experience problems and be unable to initiate sessions, even when all other clients connect successfully.

OBJECTIVES

6.15 Remotely administer servers by using Terminal Services

TERMINAL SERVICES • REMOTE ADMINSTRATION

UNDERSTANDING THE OBJECTIVE

Administration of network servers can become an overwhelming task for a single individual as a network grows. The ability to manage network servers from one location is, therefore, very appealing. Terminal Services can be used in a remote administrative mode to accomplish this goal.

WHAT YOU REALLY NEED TO KNOW

- When installed in remote administration mode, Terminal Services can be used to remotely manage a server. When Terminal Services operates in this mode, however, it cannot be used to share applications.
- To perform remote administration, you should log on to the remote system with an Administrator account.
- Nearly every administrative task can be performed through a Terminal Services session, including drive formatting, device sharing, permission setting, group policy alterations, installing drivers and software, editing the Registry, and even rebooting.
- Data can be exchanged between the Terminal Services client and the Terminal Services host (that is, the remote system).
- Cluster servers support Terminal Services only in remote administration mode.
- You must remove and then reinstall Terminal Services to switch from one mode to another.

OBJECTIVES ON THE JOB

Terminal Services offers distance control over servers within your network. The ability to control other systems remotely is a benefit that most networks need to function. When used as a remote administration tool, Terminal Services exacts only a small performance degradation price when it is actually in use. Otherwise, the host system barely notices its active presence.

PRACTICE TEST QUESTIONS

1. **Which mode of Terminal Services is supported by cluster servers?**
   a. Application sharing
   b. Remote control
   c. Remote administration
   d. Administration management center

2. **Most administrative tasks that can be performed on a local machine can also be performed remotely through Terminal Services.**
   a. True
   b. False

3. **When used in remote administration mode, Terminal Services offers complete system management control over all user accounts.**
   a. True
   b. False

4. **Assuming that all of the items listed below are present on the remote system, which of the following cannot be accessed or performed through Terminal Services? (Choose all that apply.)**
   a. Recovery Console
   b. Formatting a drive
   c. Advanced boot options
   d. CMOS
   e. Change drive letters
   f. Defragment a hard drive

5. **Both memory-resident data and data files can be transferred between a client and server within a Terminal Services session through the cut-and-paste feature of the Clipboard.**
   a. True
   b. False

6. **How is Terminal Services switched from one mode to another?**
   a. By making a selection upon start-up from the Advanced Boot Options
   b. Through the Terminal Services' Properties dialog
   c. By removing and then reinstalling Terminal Services
   d. By reinstalling Windows 2000

7. **Which common feature of Windows 2000 networks must be used to transfer files from a client to a server within a Terminal Services session?**
   a. Folder redirection
   b. Offline files
   c. Cut-and-paste
   d. Network shares

OBJECTIVES

6.16 Configure Terminal Services for application sharing

TERMINAL SERVICES • APPLICATION SHARING • APPLICATION SERVER MODE

UNDERSTANDING THE OBJECTIVE

Application sharing allows multiple low-end clients to take advantage of powerful software operating on a Terminal Services server. A connected client can reap the benefits of a high-end system even when its own local platform (operating system) does not support the application or software.

WHAT YOU REALLY NEED TO KNOW

- To share applications, Terminal Services must be installed in application server mode.
- In addition to having the system use Terminal Services, the License Manager must be installed and configured within 90 days of the application server's installation. The License Manager is installed as a Windows component through Add/Remove Programs.
- The host computer on which Terminal Services will run in application server mode must be a fairly powerful system. It also needs a lot of additional RAM. For each connected user, 3 to 9 MB of RAM is consumed based on that user's activities. This per-user RAM is in addition to the 128 MB recommended as the minimum for the host system.
- When Terminal Services is installed, it adds new features or can take advantage of latent features in Active Directory Users and Computers, System Monitor, Task Manager, and Add/Remove Programs.
- You can view and manage Terminal Services sessions through the Terminal Services Manager or from the command line.

OBJECTIVES ON THE JOB

Application sharing is a sure way to grant broad access to high-end software for low-end clients. In some cases, the use of Terminal Services is a cost-effective solution. Keep in mind, however, that the **TCO** involves purchasing user licenses and a lot of RAM and computing power on the Terminal Services host.

PRACTICE TEST QUESTIONS

1. **New drafting software costs more than $9000 per installation, but user licenses cost only $400 each. Which of the following scenarios is the most cost-effective solution for granting 10 users access to the drafting application?**
   a. Install the drafting software on 10 client workstations.
   b. Install the drafting software on a Windows 2000 Server system that has 96 MB of RAM. Use Terminal Services to grant 10 client workstations the ability to access the drafting software host system.
   c. Install the drafting software on a Windows 2000 Server system that has 512 MB of RAM. Use Terminal Services to grant 10 client workstations the ability to access the drafting software host system.
   d. There is no cost-effective solution to this situation.
2. **In addition to installing Terminal Services on the Windows 2000 Server system on which the drafting software will be installed, what other component or software must be installed to comply with all legal requirements?**
   a. Active Directory
   b. Service packs
   c. Antivirus software
   d. License Manager
   e. Network Monitor driver
3. **Microsoft requires that licensing be completed within 120 days of installing Terminal Services as an application server.**
   a. True
   b. False
4. **Which native component of Windows 2000 Server offers additional options or features when used in conjunction with Terminal Services? (Choose all that apply.)**
   a. Network and Dial-up Connections
   b. Active Directory Users and Computers
   c. System Monitor
   d. Routing and Remote Access
   e. Task Manager
   f. Network Monitor
   g. Add/Remove Programs
5. **You've installed Terminal Services on a Windows 2000 Server system with only 96 MB of RAM. You quickly discover that the system performs very poorly. You convince your manager that an additional 512 MB of RAM is essential. After installing the additional memory, how many remote users with a moderate activity level can the system support?**
   a. 10
   b. 25
   c. 64
   d. 128

OBJECTIVES

6.17 Configure applications for use with Terminal Services

TERMINAL SERVICES APPLICATION CONFIGURATION

UNDERSTANDING THE OBJECTIVE

Sharing applications from a host server to all connected clients is the purpose of Terminal Services. Many programs, however, must be specifically configured to function in a multisession environment.

WHAT YOU REALLY NEED TO KNOW

- Most applications must be configured specifically to function in a multisession environment, or they may not function properly.
- Applications for use within Terminal Services sessions must be installed on the Terminal Services host system. This installation can be carried out through Add/Remove Programs, Windows Installer, or an installation tool supplied by the software vendor.
- In all cases, the software should be installed on a system-wide basis instead of on a specific user's computer.
- Terminal Services cannot support published software (for example, as does IntelliMirror) or software installed for use only by a specific user.
- Some applications require additional configuration to function properly. Some configuration scripts are included with Terminal Services, where they are stored in the %systemroot%\Application Compatibility Scripts\Install\ folder. You should use these scripts before activating the application within Terminal Services. More information on these scripts appears in the Client Services section of the Windows 2000 Server manual.
- To ensure that an application is installed for all users, enter the command change user /install on the command line, install the application, and then enter the command change user /execute on the command line.
- You should avoid using Win16 applications whenever possible. Win16 applications require up to 40% more resources than Win32 applications.
- Most applications that are installed and configured to work in a multisession environment may need to be reinstalled after removal of Terminal Services.

OBJECTIVES ON THE JOB

The only real difficulties that you may experience with application sharing under Terminal Services relate to those applications not specifically designed for multisession use but rather for multiple-user environments. Applications that do not recognize differences between users offer no resistance when they are employed with Terminal Services.

PRACTICE TEST QUESTIONS

1. **When installing applications for use by Terminal Services clients, which of the following installation methods should you use? (Choose all that apply.)**
   a. Install the application before Terminal Services is installed.
   b. Install the application through Windows Installer.
   c. Install the application for the Administrator user account.
   d. Install the application through Add/Remove Programs.
   e. Install the application through an installation tool supplied by the software vendor.
   f. Install the application through IntelliMirror.
2. **After removal of Terminal Services, what is the recommended process for working with applications previously used through Terminal Services?**
   a. Reinstall Windows 2000 Server.
   b. Reinstall Terminal Services in remote administration mode.
   c. Remove and then reinstall the application.
   d. No action is necessary.
3. **Applications automatically function properly when used in conjunction with Terminal Services.**
   a. True
   b. False
4. **Which command can be issued on the command line to ensure that applications are installed for the entire system instead of just a single user account?**
   a. net user /change
   b. change user/ install
   c. terminal install
   d. ipconfig /all
5. **Which types of application should you avoid as much as possible because of the severe demands it places on system resources?**
   a. Multiuser applications
   b. Windows 2000 applications
   c. Windows 16-bit applications
   d. Applications without multiuser or multisession programming
6. **You can use some applications after a special configuration script is executed. Terminal Services comes equipped with many scripts for common or popular programs.**
   a. True
   b. False
7. **Applications should be reinstalled after ______________. (Choose all that apply.)**
   a. Terminal Services is installed
   b. Terminal Services is removed
   c. A new Terminal Services client is configured
   d. Running a configuration script

OBJECTIVES

6.18 Install, configure, and troubleshoot network adapters and drivers

NETWORK COMPONENT INSTALLATION AND TROUBLESHOOTING

UNDERSTANDING THE OBJECTIVE

Network adapters or **NICs** are installed and managed in much the same manner as any other hardware device. Windows 2000 automatically handles most of the complexity of linking a device with a driver and protocols to services.

WHAT YOU REALLY NEED TO KNOW

- Once a NIC is installed, Windows 2000 automatically creates a local connection object for that adapter in the Network and Dial-up Connections utility. The new connection object has all possible bindings enabled by default.
- You can configure a network adapter either through the local connection object's properties or through the Device Manager. The configuration settings offered are specific to each device, vendor, and driver. You can set system resources, such as I/O range and IRQ, for most adapters.
- Drivers can be updated or replaced from the Drivers tab of an adapter's properties sheet.
- If a bad driver is installed (through replacement or upgrade), you can restore the previous driver in many cases by rebooting using the **LKGC** (but only if you have not rebooted and logged on since installation of the bad driver).
- In cases where a NIC fails to function, it should be deleted/removed from the system through the Device Manager. After a reboot, allow the system to redetect and reinstall drivers for the device.
- If a conflict exists between a network adapter and some other device, the conflict is identified on the Resources tab of the NIC's properties dialog. In most cases, the Network Troubleshooter offers a solution. It usually results in either removal of one of the devices, moving of one of the devices to a different bus slot, or resetting of the devices' resources (that is, I/O range and IRQ).
- You should work with only 100% Windows-compatible devices.

OBJECTIVES ON THE JOB

Network adapter management under Windows 2000 is easily handled. Most of the installation is automated through Plug and Play. Most troubleshooting revolves around altering resource settings or installing updated drivers.

PRACTICE TEST QUESTIONS

1. **Which of the following is true? (Choose all that apply.)**
   a. Every time a network adapter is physically installed into a computer, you must manually install the drivers under Windows 2000.
   b. Often, when the system includes an HCL-listed network adapter, Windows 2000 automatically detects and installs drivers for it.
   c. Network adapters never conflict with other devices present in a computer.
   d. When resources are configured for use by two devices, one of the devices must be reconfigured to take advantage of other resources.
2. **When a network adapter is physically installed in a computer, which of the following items occurs automatically? (Choose all that apply.)**
   a. Plug and Play attempts to install drivers.
   b. A network connection object is created (if drivers are installed).
   c. All resource conflicts are resolved.
   d. A static IP address is assigned.
3. **Only HCL-compatible network devices can be used with Windows 2000.**
   a. True
   b. False
4. **When a network interface fails to operate, which of the following is a valid solution? (Choose all that apply.)**
   a. Move the NIC to a different bus slot.
   b. Remove the driver and then reboot.
   c. Upgrade the driver.
   d. Reinstall Windows 2000.
   e. Restore the previous settings through the LKGC.
   f. Set the IRQ to match that of the first COM port.
   g. Remove a conflicting device.
5. **A network adapter can be configured through which tool? (Choose all that apply.)**
   a. Network and Dial-Up Connections
   b. Routing and Remote Access
   c. System applet
   d. Device Manager
6. **When resources conflicts occur, Windows 2000 offers solution options through its Network Troubleshooter.**
   a. True
   b. False

Section 7

Implementing, Monitoring, and Troubleshooting Security

OBJECTIVES

7.1 Encrypt data on a hard disk by using EFS

SECURE • ENCRYPTION • PUBLIC AND PRIVATE KEY PAIRS

UNDERSTANDING THE OBJECTIVE

Windows 2000 introduces an EFS that works in conjunction with the NTFS (version 5) file system to secure data on disk media. Users who take advantage of this feature will enjoy seamless and transparent use of their files without having to constantly encrypt and decrypt their files so as to gain access—the case with other encryption systems. This step occurs automatically when the user, or a Windows application, requires access to the file's contents.

WHAT YOU REALLY NEED TO KNOW

- EFS uses symmetric and asymmetric key encryption (also known as public key technology) to encrypt files. Users who encrypt files receive a digital certificate and a public/private key pair.
- Although a user can encrypt files on local and remote machines, EFS cannot be used to encrypt data as it traverses a network. You can, however, use **SSL** or IPSec for this purpose.
- EFS works only with the NTFS file system, with one exception: If Windows Backup is used to back up files and folders, the encryption attribute will be preserved regardless of the storage media and the file system in use.
- When EFS first encrypts a file or folder, a designated recovery agent must be present on the system. By default, EFS sets the local administrator account (on stand-alone machines), or the domain administrator (for the first domain controller that was installed in a domain), as the recovery agent. Alternative recovery agents can be specified, depending on the recovery agent policy implementation.
- Windows 2000 file encryption is account-specific.
- EFS maintains the private key in the user's profile.

OBJECTIVES ON THE JOB

A pertinent point when dealing with EFS relates to the effects of moving and copying files. Fundamentally, this operation is much the same as with compression; put another way, a file copied into an encrypted folder inherits the encryption attribute, whereas a file moved in the same way does not. Therefore, moving an encrypted file into an unencrypted folder preserves the encryption on the file. Moreover, EFS does not affect other file permissions, so an Administrator can still delete a file encrypted by another user. Finally, encryption will be lost if files and folders do not reside on the NTFS file system.

PRACTICE TEST QUESTIONS

Kim, a Windows 2000 Professional user, wants to place some sensitive files in a subdirectory of her home folder called Private; the home folder resides on a network file server. She does not want anyone else to view these files. Kim also wants to access her files from other Windows 2000 client machines on her office network. Currently, Kim logs on to the office network from her personal machine.

1. **How can Kim secure her sensitive files?**
    a. By using NTFS file permissions
    b. By using the Encrypting File System
    c. This cannot be done without third-party software.
    d. By ensuring that the Private folder and any files to be secured reside on Kim's local machine and then using IPSec technology to secure them
2. **Kim wants to encrypt all of the files she places in the Private folder and any subsequent files she copies there. What is her best option?**
    a. Encrypt the Private folder and the files it contains separately. Encrypt any files and folders that are placed within the Private folder individually before moving them.
    b. Encrypt the home folder, but select the "Only encrypt child directories" option on the folder's properties sheet.
    c. Encrypt the home folders only.
    d. Encrypt the Private folder only.
3. **How can Kim access her encrypted files from other client computers on the office network?**
    a. Kim should set up a roaming profile for herself.
    b. Kim should ask the network administrator to configure a roaming profile for her.
    c. Kim should select the "Enable roaming access" option when first encrypting the files and folders.
    d. This task cannot be done; encrypted files can be accessed only locally.
4. **Kim leaves the company without reversing the encryption in the Private folder. You need to access the contents of the files stored there. How could you proceed? (Choose all that apply.)**
    a. Use the cipher /d [decrypt] /f [force] command.
    b. Log on as the Administrator and recover the files and folders.
    c. Back up the files and folders and move them to another folder.
    d. Set the NTFS permissions of the file to read and write.
5. **Which file system can be employed along with the Encrypting File System?**
    a. NTFS
    b. NTFS version 5
    c. FAT
    d. FAT32

OBJECTIVES

7.2 Implement and configure policies in a Windows 2000 environment

GROUP POLICY • ACTIVE DIRECTORY

UNDERSTANDING THE OBJECTIVE

Another addition to the Windows 2000 feature set is the group policy, which in essence is a grown-up version of the Windows NT 4.0 system policies. **GP** allows for centralized control of users and computers that can be altered only by system administrators—a significant improvement over Windows NT 4.0 system policies, which could be changed by a savvy user. GP is complex, especially when combined with AD, as it should be to gain maximum administrative effect. Because it is powerful, it warrants careful scrutiny.

WHAT YOU REALLY NEED TO KNOW

- ◆ GP is made up of GPOs, which are themselves AD-based objects that allow for the centralized management of Windows 2000 users and computers.
- ◆ A **GPO** is a physical system policy that you correlate to a domain, site, or **OU**. In Windows NT 4.0, it consists of the NTCONFIG.POL file; with physical GPOs, it encompasses both files and AD objects.
- ◆ GP supports a broad array of user and machine configurations, such as the following: Registry-based policy settings; security for local and domain-wide machines; software deployment utilizing Windows Installer Technology; logon and logoff scripts; and start-up/shutdown scripts.
- ◆ The MMC administers GPOs. Add the Active Directory Users and Computers (for domains and OUs) and Active Directory Sites and Services (for sites) snap-ins to the MMC to set up this administrative model.
- ◆ GPOs can be managed either locally or remotely. Administrative privileges are required to perform this operation, however.
- ◆ The Windows 2000 system handles the replication of system policies. Policies can be stored either in AD or locally. On stand-alone machines, only a locally stored local computer policy exists.

OBJECTIVES ON THE JOB

Coming to grips with GP can be a daunting task. It is far superior to anything provided by Windows NT 4.0 system policies and gives the administrator far more granular control over user and computer settings. GPOs are not user profiles, however, and they do not affect security groups. The full capabilities of GPOs are realized by their implementation within AD so as to facilitate centralized computer and user management. All Windows 2000 machines still have a local computer policy that may or may not be overridden by settings found higher in the configuration hierarchy (discussed in Objective 7.3).

PRACTICE TEST QUESTIONS

1. **What is a group policy object?**
    a. A system policy
    b. A system policy that utilizes the NTCONFIG.POL file to store its settings
    c. A physical system policy that can be associated with a site, domain, or organizational unit
    d. A user profile that is stored in Active Directory
2. **How are group policies administered in Windows 2000?**
    a. By using the Group Policy Service
    b. From the Group Policy Control Panel applet
    c. From My Computer | Group Policy Settings
    d. By using the Microsoft Management Console
3. **What can you type in the Run dialog to activate the Group Policy Editor?**
    a. Gpedit.msc
    b. Grppol.mmc
    c. Gpedit.mmc
    d. Grppol.msc
4. **Which service is responsible for replicating group policies?**
    a. File Replication Service
    b. Group Policy Replication Service
    c. Replicator Service
    d. Netlogon Service
5. **For what purpose can you use a group policy? (Choose all that apply.)**
    a. Software deployment
    b. Logon/logoff scripts
    c. Start-up/shutdown scripts
    d. Security settings
    e. Registry-based policy settings
    f. User profiles
    g. Security group configuration
6. **Sue, a group policy systems administrator for a prominent software company, needs to configure a stand-alone machine outside the Active Directory-based group policy objects that are in force in the domain's organizational unit. How can she accomplish this task?**
    a. In the Run dialog, type mmc and add the Group Policy snap-in. Make the necessary configuration changes.
    b. In the Run dialog, type mmc and add the Local Policy snap-in. Make the necessary configuration changes.
    c. This configuration is not possible. Only machines within the Active Directory-based group policy object can be given group policies.
    d. As a local user working interactively, in the Run dialog, type gpedit.msc and configure the required settings.

OBJECTIVES

7.3 Manage group policies in a Windows 2000 environment

GROUP POLICY OBJECTS • PROCESSING OPTIONS

UNDERSTANDING THE OBJECTIVE

The management of GPs in Windows 2000 is a complex affair. GPs allow you to fully customize the appearance of users' desktops and can affect their user profiles. GP configuration and arrangement can be tricky—without the comprehensive knowledge of the GP's inner workings, the application of settings for users and computers is likely to be an erroneous exercise.

WHAT YOU REALLY NEED TO KNOW

- A GP is applied in the following order: local computer policy, site-linked GPOs, domain-linked GPOs, and OU-linked GPOs.
- If multiple GPOs link to the same site, domain, or OU, they will be applied in order of their priority, with the highest in the list taking precedence.
- GP uses processing options to determine how to enforce policies within sites, domains, and OUs.
- Using GPO-level processing options, you can disable computer and user configuration settings for a GPO object that links to any site, domain, or OU.
- Another GPO-level method of controlling the application of GPOs involves security groups. When a user logs on, Windows 2000 determines whether that user has permission to read a GPO. The Read and Apply Group Policy permissions are required for a user to access any particular GPO.
- Three types of link-level processing options exist: Block Policy Inheritance, No Override, and Disabled. These processing options apply only to the immediate site, domain, or OU to which the GPO links.
- Using the Block Policy Inheritance setting at the site, domain, or OU level (this setting cannot be applied to GPOs) prevents the application of higher-level group policies.
- The No Override setting is used to enforce a GPO in a site, domain, or OU, regardless of other settings such as Block Policy Inheritance; it overrides the other settings.

OBJECTIVES ON THE JOB

Unfortunately, there are no shortcuts in learning to appreciate the niceties of group policies in Windows 2000. Understanding the basic concepts of GPs will aid you when configuring group policy in an organization. Nevertheless, nothing beats hands-on experience—especially in this instance, where familiarity with the nuances of Windows 2000's group policy specifications can be attained only through physical trial and error.

PRACTICE TEST QUESTIONS

1. **A user logs on to a Windows 2000 domain where group policies are in force. In what order will group policies be applied?**
   a. Local computer policy, site-linked GPOs, domain-linked GPOs, OU-linked GPOs
   b. Local computer policy, site-linked GPOs, OU-linked GPOs, domain-linked GPOs
   c. Local computer policy, domain-linked GPOs, OU-linked GPOs, site-linked GPOs
   d. OU-linked GPOs, domain-linked GPOs, site-linked GPOs, local computer policy
2. **Paul, a group policy administrator, created a new site-level GPO that contains only computer settings. He wants to speed up the process for users when they log on to use this policy. How can he do so?**
   a. Select the Disable Computer Configuration Settings check box in the site-level GPO's properties
   b. Select the Disable User Configuration settings check box in the site-level GPO's properties
   c. On each machine that will use the policy, create a local computer policy that enforces computer settings only
   d. Create a domain-wide group policy stipulating that only computer settings should be loaded when a user logs on and connects to Active Directory
3. **An audit of the Accounts Department is currently under way in a global software company. As a group policy administrator, you need to give the outside auditors the same desktop configurations that the Accounts Department uses. All users in the Accounts Department belong to the Accountants group. How can this setup be achieved?**
   a. Add the auditors to the Accounts group
   b. Add the auditors to the Domain Admins group
   c. Add the auditors to the Accountants group
   d. Create a new GPO that mirrors the Accounts Department's group policy, create a new group called Outside Auditors, and give this group read and write permissions to the newly created GPO
4. **Sharon, a group policy administrator, must create a specific policy for the Graphics OU that gives those users custom background wallpaper on their desktops without affecting other users outside this OU. Currently, the sites, domains, and OUs in her large enterprise employ a corporate logo for the desktop wallpaper. How can she implement this change?**
   a. Create a new GPO for the Graphics OU and apply the No Override setting to it.
   b. Create a new GPO for the Graphics OU and apply the Block Policy Inheritance setting to it.
   c. Create a new GPO for the Graphics OU and apply the Do Not Block Policy Inheritance setting to it.

OBJECTIVES

7.4 Troubleshoot policies in a Windows 2000 environment

CONFLICTS • DIAGNOSIS • LOGGING • UTILITIES

UNDERSTANDING THE OBJECTIVE

Because GP is so multifaceted, it would be surprising if you did not encounter troubleshooting issues. Numerous things can go awry in a GP configuration, especially in large, multidomain organizations. Attempting to unravel the mysteries of complex GP settings can be an onerous affair, but good comprehension of the subject matter goes a long way in lessening this task.

WHAT YOU REALLY NEED TO KNOW

- If scripts configured in a GP do not run, verify that the user has the GP Scripts extension applied to his or her computer or that replication has occurred in either AD or the FRS for the domain controller in use.
- If the application of Registry settings using administrative templates is unsuccessful on users' computers in GP, this problem might be caused by failing DNS, an inability to connect to a **DC**, or incomplete AD replication on the DC in use.
- If you cannot open a GPO, determine whether you have write permission for the GPO and confirm that the DC to which you are connected is online.
- If a user logs on and experiences unexpected behavior in a multidomain environment, ensure that complex replication has occurred for Active Directory and the Sysvol.
- Sometimes a user who is managed by GP logs on to the network but does not receive the GP settings, while every other user does. Possible causes of this problem include the following issues: the user is logged on from a non-Windows 2000 machine; loopback is in effect, so the user GP is replaced by the computer GP; or disk quota enforcement is in place, preventing the GP from running because the disk space is needed by other services.
- Inheritance issues can produce unexpected results in the application of GP for users. Things to watch for include the order in which GPOs have been applied, as policies set later ordinarily take precedence; the GPO's No Override issues and use of the Block Policy Inheritance feature; and disabling of the GPO, or a user or computer part of a GP.

OBJECTIVES ON THE JOB

At this stage, you may think that correcting an erroneous group policy configuration in either a single-domain or multidomain environment is akin to picking a needle out of a haystack. Microsoft has provided some useful tools to assist in this troubleshooting—namely, NETDIAG.EXE and REPLMON.EXE. Moreover, you can enable verbose logging to assist further in GP fault diagnosis. This feature tracks all changes made by GP and its extensions on the local computer. Enabling this feature requires a trip to the Registry to add the UserenvDebugLevel value.

PRACTICE TEST QUESTIONS

1. **Susie, a trainee group policy administrator in a multidomain environment, wants to apply the Block Policy Inheritance setting to a group policy object that she just created, but she cannot find this option. Why?**
   a. She has insufficient administrative privileges.
   b. She does not have the Apply Group Policy Inheritance rights for the account with which she is currently logged on.
   c. This setting cannot be applied to group policy objects.
   d. She is not looking diligently enough—it's located in the Options dialog of the group policy object, not in the properties dialog.
2. **You need to update a Registry entry on all of your users' computers in a local area network. Group policies are in force throughout the Windows 2000 environment. How can you apply the update with the least amount of administrative effort?**
   a. Create a new group policy object and add a preconfigured INF file to it.
   b. Create a new group policy object and add a preconfigured ADM template to it.
   c. Configure an ADM template and add it to the users' logon scripts.
   d. Users' Registry settings cannot be change through a group policy.
3. **Tom, a Windows 2000 Professional user, logs on to the network and experiences strange occurrences, resulting in a desktop that does not appear to function correctly. Group policies are enabled in his exclusively Windows 2000 multidomain environment. What is the most likely cause of the problem? (Choose two.)**
   a. Changes to the Sysvol have not yet been replicated
   b. Changes to Active Directory have not yet been replicated
   c. Full synchronization has not occurred in the SAM database
   d. Full synchronization has not occurred in the NETLOGON share
4. **Group policies are enabled in a pure Windows 2000 environment, which includes a Seattle site, a Corporate domain, and two Finance and Marketing organizational units. Although you create a new group policy object in the Finance OU that specifies a logon message, it is not applied when the Finance OU users log on. Why?**
   a. The users in the Finance OU have a local computer policy that overrides the new group policy object.
   b. A domain-level group policy object stipulates another logon message.
   c. A site-level group policy object stipulates another logon message.
   d. A domain-level group policy object stipulates another logon message that has the No Override setting applied to it.

OBJECTIVES

7.5 Implement, configure, manage, and troubleshoot Local Policy in a Windows 2000 environment

NODES • GROUP POLICY OBJECTS • CONFLICTS

UNDERSTANDING THE OBJECTIVE

On some occasions, an enterprise GP may not for a particular computer (for example, a kiosk-based computer). Accordingly the need exists, perhaps, for a locally focused group policy. A local group policy then becomes the controlling influence over the stand-alone computer configuration.

WHAT YOU REALLY NEED TO KNOW

- Two types of GPOs exist: local and nonlocal. Only one GPO is located on any individual Windows 2000 computer. Nonlocal GPOs reside in AD.
- The local GPO is stored in the %systemroot%\System32\GroupPolicy directory. Only the nodes under Security Settings are configured by default. Other nodes under the GPO are not configured (neither enabled nor disabled).
- **DACLs** can be used to set permissions on the GroupPolicy directory, thereby enabling an Administrator to control which users are affected by the local policy. By default, Administrators have full control to this folder. If the read permission is removed, access will not be permitted to this directory, so the policy will not affect Administrators.
- To manage GP on a stand-alone machine, you must add the Group Policy snap-in to the MMC.
- Remote computer management can be implemented by browsing to any such machine while adding the snap-in to create the necessary focus. Note that the Security Settings extension does not support remote management.
- Local GPOs are always processed first, followed by nonlocal GPOs. By default, if a conflict occurs between the two, the nonlocal GPO always prevails. If a computer withdraws from participation in a domain, the local GPO is reapplied.

OBJECTIVES ON THE JOB

At this point, some mention of Windows 2000 policy files is in order. Known as REGISTRY.POL files in Windows 2000, they are akin to Windows 9x CONFIG.POL files and Windows NT 4.0 NTCONFIG.POL files. The administrative template extension of GP saves these files to the \Machine and \User subdirectories for computer and user settings, respectively. They contain the customized settings for each aforementioned group. Windows 2000 policy files are text files with embedded binary strings, whereas Windows 9x and NT 4.0 policy files are purely binary in nature.

PRACTICE TEST QUESTIONS

1. **What is a type of group policy objects? (Choose all that apply.)**
   a. Local
   b. Nonlocal
   c. Remote
   d. Nonremote
2. **Where is the local group policy object stored on a stand-alone computer?**
   a. %systemroot%\System32\Policies
   b. %systemroot%\System\GroupPolicy
   c. %systemroot%\System32\GroupPolicy
   d. %systemroot%\GroupPolicy
3. **Which node of the local group policy object is configured by default? (Choose all that apply.)**
   a. Software Settings
   b. Security Settings
   c. Administrative Templates
   d. Windows Settings
4. **John works for a large Internet bookseller. He has configured a stand-alone Windows 2000 machine with a custom group policy in the warehouse, so that employees can access certain information. He wants only warehouse staff to have this custom policy—not members of management, who may also use this machine. How could he achieve this goal?**
   a. Create a new group containing only the management employees and give this group the relevant permissions to load the custom group policy.
   b. Create a new group containing only the warehouse employees and give this group the relevant permissions to load the custom group policy.
   c. Create a new group containing only the warehouse employees and give this group the relevant permissions to load the custom group policy; also, ensure that the Read permission is removed from the Authenticated Users and Administrators groups for this group policy.
   d. You cannot control group access through a local group policy. Make the computer into a member of an Active Directory-based group policy domain.
5. **Mary, a trainee group policy administrator for a large software company, is attempting to configure group policy on a remote machine. She loaded the Group Policy snap-in and browsed to the correct computer, but cannot manage the Security Settings extension of the local group policy object on the remote machine. Other nodes are available to configure. Why?**
   a. Remote Security Settings management is not supported.
   b. Mary has a network connectivity problem.
   c. A nonlocal group policy object is taking precedence.
   d. A name resolution problem is present, most likely with the DNS settings, which affect only the Security Settings because they are the only ones configured by default.

OBJECTIVES

7.6 Implement, configure, manage, and troubleshoot System Policy in a Windows 2000 environment

SYSTEM POLICY EDITOR • POLICY FILES • TEMPLATES

UNDERSTANDING THE OBJECTIVE

Although we have explored group policy in detail, sometimes Windows NT 4.0 and/or 9x system policies must either coexist with a Windows 2000 group policy or be the sole implementation controlling users' desktops. Therefore, some understanding of these environments is required—not just for the Microsoft exam, but also for the real world.

WHAT YOU REALLY NEED TO KNOW

- Windows 2000 group policy does not support Windows NT 4.0 or 9x clients, despite the availability of AD support for these clients.
- Windows NT 4.0-based clients can be managed with administrative (.adm) templates (in the group policy) and the Windows NT 4.0 System Policy Editor (poledit.exe; – a GUI-based program) in a Windows 2000 domain.
- The Windows 2000 SPE provides policy support for Windows 9x users, which creates policy (.pol) files.
- Windows NT 4.0 uses the NTCONFIG.POL file and Windows 9x uses the CONFIG.POL file.
- Once policy files are created under the relevant operating system, you must copy them to the domain's NETLOGON share, which is located in different areas depending on the operating system in use. Under Windows 2000, use %systemroot%\SYSVOL\sysvol\ <domain name>\SCRIPTS; under NT 4.0, use %systemroot%\winnt\system32 \Repl\Import\Scripts.
- The Windows 2000 **SPE** must be run locally on Windows 9x clients to create the correct and compatible CONFIG.POL files.
- Windows 2000 .adm files can be used only with the SPE supplied with Windows 2000, because Windows 2000 SPE now supports Unicode-encoded .adm files.

OBJECTIVES ON THE JOB

In some instances, Windows NT 4.0 system policy must be present in conjunction with Windows 2000 group policy. For example, this setup is necessary for a Windows 2000 Professional client machine with Windows NT 4.0 domain controllers that are in the process of being migrated to Windows 2000. In this environment, user and computer accounts may exist on differing domains, so the location of these accounts influences the resulting enforced user and machine configuration.

PRACTICE TEST QUESTIONS

1. **For which client does Windows 2000 group policy provide support?**
   a. Windows 3.x
   b. Windows 9.x
   c. Windows NT 4.0
   d. Windows 2000
2. **Tom, a systems administrator for a multinational software company, is in the process of migrating a Windows NT 4.0 network to Windows 2000. In the interim, he needs to manage Windows NT 4.0 system policies from Windows 2000 domain controllers. How can he do so? (Choose all that apply.)**
   a. Tom should upgrade the clients to Windows 2000 Server so that they can participate in group policy.
   b. Tom can use the Windows NT 4.0 System Policy Editor to create policy files that are placed on the Windows 2000 domain controllers.
   c. Tom can implement administrative templates in group policy.
   d. Tom should place the NTCONFIG.POL file in the Windows 2000 group policy.
3. **Sue wants to create Windows 9x system policies for a Windows 2000 domain. How can she implement this environment?**
   a. Run the Windows 2000 System Policy Editor on the Windows 9x clients locally to create a CONFIG.POL file.
   b. Run the Windows 2000 System Policy Editor on the Windows 9x clients remotely to create a CONFIG.POL file.
   c. Run the Windows 9x System Policy Editor on the Windows 9x clients locally to create a CONFIG.POL file.
   d. Run the Windows 9x System Policy Editor on the Windows 9x clients remotely to create a CONFIG.POL file.
4. **You are in charge of an enterprise consisting of only Windows 2000 Servers that participate in a domain. Currently, all clients run either Windows NT 4.0 or 9x and had system policies implemented when the domain controllers were based on Windows NT 4.0. How can you maintain the old system policies in the Windows 2000 domain?**
   a. Add a mapping in each user's logon script that points to the policy (.pol) file in the NETLOGON share.
   b. Place the relevant operating system clients' system policy files in the NETLOGON share of the Windows 2000 domain controllers.
   c. Windows 2000 group policy does not support earlier versions of Windows, so the only way to control the legacy clients' desktops is to upgrade them to Windows 2000 Professional.
   d. Install a Windows NT 4.0 domain controller on the network, copy the Windows NT 4.0 and 9x policy files to the NETLOGON share, and replicate it to the NETLOGON share on the Windows 2000 domain controllers.

OBJECTIVES

7.7 Implement, configure, manage, and troubleshoot auditing

AUDIT • SECURITY LOG ACTIVITIES

UNDERSTANDING THE OBJECTIVE

Windows 2000 comes with a comprehensive array of built-in auditing capabilities. Such a feature is useful because it means that a wide variety of events can be tracked and monitored on a network. This effort can safeguard the network from potential problems and unauthorized access attempts.

WHAT YOU REALLY NEED TO KNOW

- Auditing can be used to log an event whenever a file or folder is accessed or particular actions are executed. For each action, a log entry is written to the Security Log in Event Viewer.
- You can audit the success or failure of an action, with the audit trail identifying who was successful at a certain action and who attempted but failed at any particular event.
- Although auditing is native to Windows 2000, it is not enabled by default.
- Numerous types of events can be audited: account logon events, account management, directory service access, logon events, object access, policy change, privilege use, process tracking, and system events.
- Audit policies are affected by group policy inheritance. Thus local computer audit policies can be overridden by domain group policies in certain circumstances.
- Once auditing is enabled, you must configure what is actually audited on certain objects, such as printers, files, and folders.

OBJECTIVES ON THE JOB

Activating auditing in Windows 2000 can have implications for the size of the Security Log in Event Viewer. Without control, it can become quite large in a short period of time, affecting your overall available disk space. Event Viewer allows you to control the size of the Security Log and dictate how events are written. You can set a maximum size for the Security Log and specify whether it should be overwritten as needed, after *n* days, or not at all (in which case, you can clear the log manually). You can even stop a Windows 2000 Server when the Security Log becomes full by using a help file-documented Registry edit.

PRACTICE TEST QUESTIONS

Senior management has asked Dawn to track users' access to files and folders on her Windows 2000 network. The network consists of one domain with member servers as well as domain controllers that participate in group policy.

1. **Auditing in Windows 2000 is enabled by default.**
    a. True
    b. False
2. **How is auditing enabled?**
    a. By default
    b. In the relevant GPO in the MMC
    c. In the Control Panel, Auditing applet
    d. In the Auditing of Users snap-in for the MMC
3. **What are the fundamental steps that Dawn must execute when configuring auditing in Windows 2000? (Choose all that apply.)**
    a. Turn on event categories that need to be audited.
    b. Specify the size and behavior of the Security Log.
    c. If account logon events access or account management access has been selected, set the Success and Failure attributes as required.
    d. If directory service access or object access has been selected, set the Success and Failure attributes as required.
4. **How does group policy inheritance affect Dawn's local auditing on a Windows 2000 Server?**
    a. Local policy auditing and group policy auditing are independent of each other and therefore have no effect on one another.
    b. If a group policy stipulates an audit policy that conflicts with a local audit policy, group policy will prevail.
    c. If a group policy stipulates an audit policy that conflicts with a local audit policy, local policy will prevail.
    d. If local and group policy audit policies are in place, both will be used for auditing.
5. **On which volumes can Dawn configure auditing for files and folders? (Choose all that apply.)**
    a. FAT16
    b. FAT32
    c. NTFS v.4
    d. NTFS v.5
6. **Which Security Log file options are available to Dawn in the Event Viewer when she is configuring the log file? (Choose all that apply.)**
    a. Overwrite events as needed
    b. Overwrite events older than *n* days
    c. Do not overwrite events (clear log manually)
    d. Maximum log size

OBJECTIVES

7.8 Implement, configure, manage, and troubleshoot local accounts

WORKSTATION AND DOMAIN ACCOUNTS • SAM

UNDERSTANDING THE OBJECTIVE

Ordinarily, Windows 2000 domain controller security principal accounts are located in AD. Nevertheless, member and stand-alone servers often appear on a network. As these computers store their security principal accounts locally rather than in AD, some explanation of this environment is justified.

WHAT YOU REALLY NEED TO KNOW

- Windows 2000 supports two types of accounts: domain and workstation. Workstation accounts are limited to the physical computer on which they reside, which can be a workstation, member, or stand-alone server. Domain accounts extend to all computers in a domain.
- Workstation accounts reside in the **SAM** database (located in the Registry). Domain accounts reside in AD, although the SAM is retained to ensure compatibility on domain controllers.
- Two local user accounts are built into Windows 2000: Administrator and Guest. The Administrator account is used for managing the local machine and has unlimited access. Neither account can be deleted.
- Once a user account is created, it can be assigned to groups for security purposes, and user profile and home folder details can be entered into the user account properties.
- User names must be unique, cannot contain the characters " / \ [ ] : ; | = , + * ? < >, and must not be all periods and spaces. A maximum of 20 characters is permitted.
- It is far more preferable to rename an unwanted user account than to delete it, as you cannot recover a deleted account. Renaming an account will allow the account to retain its SID and all other properties.

OBJECTIVES ON THE JOB

Once you have set up a new user account, the need may arise to customize that account with a roaming or mandatory user profile or to assign a home folder to it. With roaming or mandatory profiles, note that the user profile path to the shared directory (requires full control for the Everyone group) on a server does not need a file name for Windows NT 4.0 or 2000 clients. To make a roaming profile mandatory, just rename NTUSER.DAT to NTUSER.MAN. Moreover, you can substitute the *%username%* variable for the last subdirectory in the home folder path—for example, *\\server\share\%username%*.

PRACTICE TEST QUESTIONS

Ken just installed a Windows 2000 member server that will reside in his company's New York domain. It will house top-secret company information that only senior executives of the company should be able to access interactively. Ken needs to configure accounts for those executives who also have accounts in the Windows 2000 New York domain.

1. **What type of account should Ken create on the Windows 2000 member server?**
   a. Domain
   b. Workstation
   c. Member
   d. Stand-alone
2. **Where will the accounts that Ken creates be situated?**
   a. Active Directory
   b. The Security Accounts Manager database
   c. The %systemroot% directory
   d. The %systemroot%\system32 directory
3. **Where would Ken add and configure the new user accounts that he wishes to create?**
   a. In the MMC, User Manager
   b. In the MMC, User Manager for Domains
   c. In the MMC, Computer Management
   d. In the MMC, Local User Accounts
4. **What is the maximum length in characters for a user name that can be used in this scenario?**
   a. 10
   b. 15
   c. 20
   d. 256
5. **What is the maximum password length in characters in this situation?**
   a. 14
   b. 256
   c. 128
   d. 127
6. **Ken wants the users that he creates to maintain the profiles with which they usually log on. How can he achieve this goal?**
   a. Copy their existing profiles to a network share and grant the Everyone group Full Control access to it. Specify the profile path in each user's account properties sheet.
   b. Copy their existing profiles to a network share and grant the Everyone group Full Control access to it. Specify the profile path in the logon script field in each user's account properties sheet.
   c. Change the NTUSER.DAT file's extension to .man.
   d. This task is impossible; roaming profiles can be present only on domain controllers.

OBJECTIVES

7.9 Implement, configure, manage, and troubleshoot Account Policy

ACCOUNT POLICIES • PASSWORDS • LOCKOUT • KERBEROS

UNDERSTANDING THE OBJECTIVE

Account policies can play a crucial role in the security of a Windows 2000 network. For this reason, it is essential to implement an effective account policy. Account policies define how a user account will interact with the authenticating server and can be established as part of a domain-based group policy or on stand-alone machines.

WHAT YOU REALLY NEED TO KNOW

- Account policies are configured via the MMC. The Local Computer Policy snap-in is the general location for account policy configuration. The configuration is actually found in Local Computer Policy\Computer Configuration\Windows Settings\Security Settings\Account Polices.
- Three subcategories of the Account Policies category exist: Password Policy, Account Lockout Policy, and Kerberos Policy.
- Password Policy allows you to define settings such as password length and minimum and maximum password age. In addition, you can require password complexity of users and have passwords be stored using reversible encryption.
- Kerberos Policy applies to domain user accounts. It determines such things as Kerberos ticket lifetimes and enforcement of these lifetimes.
- It is important to note that when setting account policies in AD, Windows 2000 only permits one domain account policy. The domain account policy will always take precedence over a Windows 2000 workstation or Server that is a member of the particular domain. The exception involves the presence of a defined account policy for an OU, which then prevails.

OBJECTIVES ON THE JOB

Implementing account policies is a tricky affair; on the surface, the best and most practical approach to improving security in an organization seems to be implementing a strict account policy. This approach could bring problems, however. For example, if you specify a restrictive account lockout policy, it could lead to increased denial-of-service attacks and place an extra burden on your help desk staff. Moreover, specifying a restrictive password policy can lead to looser security on the network, as users may start writing down too-long passwords. For this reason, it is best to set password length to no more than seven characters. Thus account policy maintenance is not as straightforward as it initially appears. Accordingly, a balance must be struck between the users' need for relatively easy network access and the enterprise's need for tight security.

PRACTICE TEST QUESTIONS

1. **Where do you specify the account policy on a Windows 2000 Server?**
    a. Control Panel, Account Policy applet
    b. Microsoft Management Console
    c. Administrative Tools, Account Policy
    d. Start, Settings, Account Policy Restrictions
2. **What are the three account policy subcategories in the Security Settings category?**
    a. Lockout Policy
    b. Account Lockout Policy
    c. Kerberos Policy
    d. Password Policy
3. **Which setting can you define under Password Policy when configuring an account policy in Windows 2000 Server? (Choose all that apply.)**
    a. Password history
    b. Password age
    c. Password duration
    d. Password length
4. **Which setting can you define under Account Lockout Policy when configuring an account policy in Windows 2000 Server? (Choose all that apply.)**
    a. Account lockout permissions
    b. Account lockout policy
    c. Account lockout duration
    d. Account lockout threshold
5. **You configured Kerberos account policies in your Windows 2000 domain in Active Directory. The Windows 2000 Servers are configured for mixedmode, as Windows NT 4.0 domain controllers have yet to be migrated. These specific account policies are not being applied to some Windows 2000 Professional clients, however. What could be the explanation for this problem?**
    a. Local account policy is taking precedence.
    b. Full replication of group policy has not taken place.
    c. The File Replication Service has been manually stopped.
    d. A Windows NT 4.0 BDC is authenticating the client, so the NTLM protocol is being used as the authentication mechanism.

OBJECTIVES

7.10 Implement, configure, manage, and troubleshoot security by using the Security Configuration Tool Set

SECURITY POLICIES • MONITORING • AUDIT

UNDERSTANDING THE OBJECTIVE

The **SCTS** is essentially a group of MMC snap-ins, offered as either stand-alone products or extensions, that provide the system administrator with a centralized point from which to configure security settings in a Windows network. It represents a considerable improvement over Windows NT 4.0 which makes tools available to perform the same tasks, but lacks the ability to configure security settings from a central point. Consequently, the Windows NT 4.0 administrator must open three or four management utilities to perform security configuration and management.

WHAT YOU REALLY NEED TO KNOW

- You can use the SCTS to configure security policies on a local individual computer and on a domain and organizational unit basis with group policy in the Active Directory service.
- The SCTS can be integrated with the group policy structure to extend its functionality and to provide security policies on GPOs where required.
- The SCTS allows you to manage the following security regions in Windows 2000: account policies, local policies, Event Log, restricted groups, system services, Registry, and file system.
- The following components of the SCTS can be used to manage and configure the security areas mentioned above: Security Settings extension to Group Policy; Security Configuration and Analysis snap-in; Security Templates snap-in; and SECEDIT.EXE.
- You can analyze security policies by utilizing the Security Configuration and Analysis snap-in for the MMC. All configuration and analyses are monitored through databases: Either you create a new database or open an existing database for analysis.
- The security policy analysis highlights inconsistencies by placing a white cross in a red circle icon over the relevant object. Consistencies are marked with a green tick in a white circle icon.

OBJECTIVES ON THE JOB

You must be thoroughly familiar with the SCTS, understanding its role in analyzing and maintaining security policies on stand-alone machines or in AD. The SCTS represents a considerable improvement over security policy management in earlier Windows versions. You can now readily perform corporate-wide security audits from a centralized point in Windows 2000. This ability facilitates the implementation and monitoring of overall security policy at macro and micro levels, giving the administrator a very fine level of control.

PRACTICE TEST QUESTIONS

1. **In which security areas can the Security Configuration Tool Set be implemented in Windows 2000? (Choose all that apply.)**
    a. Account policies
    b. Event Log
    c. Registry
    d. Restricted groups
    e. System services
    f. File system
    g. Local policies
2. **The Security Configuration Tool Set integrates with, and extends the functionality of, group policy objects.**
    a. True
    b. False
3. **The Security Configuration and Analysis snap-in for the Microsoft Management Console has a command-line-equivalent utility. What is it called?**
    a. SCEDIT.EXE
    b. SECEDIT.EXE
    c. SECEDITOR.EXE
    d. No such utility exists.
4. **John has performed a security analysis of a Windows 2000 member server computer. On examining the results of this analysis, he notices some discrepancies in the implemented security policies. How does John recognize this problem?**
    a. The analysis report details the discrepancies.
    b. The discrepancies are highlighted with a green tick in a white circle icon.
    c. The discrepancies are highlighted with a red cross in a white circle icon.
    d. The discrepancies are highlighted with a white cross in a red circle icon.
5. **David, a trainee systems administrator, wants to perform a security audit of a stand-alone Windows 2000 Server computer. He started the Microsoft Management Console and installed the Security Configuration and Analysis snap-in, but he can't find the option to analyze the local computer's security settings. Why?**
    a. David must create a new database.
    b. David must import a security template before proceeding further.
    c. David must right-click the snap-in and select Analyze Computer Now.
    d. The Security Configuration and Analysis snap-in can be used only for group policy in the Active Directory service.

GLOSSARY OF ACRONYMS AND ABBREVIATIONS

A

ACPI – Advanced Configuration and Power Interface
AD – Active Directory
ADIW – Active Directory Installation Wizard
ASP – Active Server Page
ATM – Asynchronous Transfer Mode

B

BAP – Bandwidth Allocation Protocol
BDC – Backup Domain Controller
BIOS – Basic Input Output System

C

CSNW – Client Services for NetWare

D

DACL – Discretionary Access Control List
DC – Domain Controller
DES – Data Encryption Standard
Dfs – Distributed File System
DLC – Data Link Control
DM – Device Manager, Disk Management
DNS – Domain Name System
DHCP – Dynamic Host Configuration Protocol

E

ERD – Emergency Repair Disk
EFS – Encrypting File System

F

FAT – File Allocation Table
FRS – File Replication Service
FTP – File Transfer Protocol

G

GP – Group Policy
GPO – Group Policy object
GSNW – Gateway Service for NetWare
GUI – Graphical User Interface

H

HAL – Hardware Abstraction Layer
HCL – Hardware Compatibility List
HTML – Hypertext Markup Language
HTTP – Hypertext Transport Protocol

I

IIS – Internet Information Services
I/O – Input/Output
IP – Internet Protocol
IPP – Internet Printing Protocol
IPSec – Internet Protocol Security
IPX – Internet Packet Exchange
IrDA – Infrared Data Association
IRQ – Interrupt Request Line
ISA – Industry Standard Architecture
ISDN – Integrated Services Digital Network
ISP – Internet Service Provider

L

L2TP – Layer 2 Tunneling Protocol
LAN – Local Area Network
LCP – Local Computer Policy
LKGC – Last Known Good Configuration

M

MMC – Microsoft Management Console
MS-CHAP – Microsoft Challenge Handshake Authentication Protocol

N

NAT – Network Address Translation
NetBEUI – NetBIOS Enhanced User Interface
NetBIOS – Network Basic Input Output System
NIC – Network Interface Card
NNTP – Network News Transport Protocol
NTFS – New Technology File System
NTVDM – NT Virtual DOS Machine
NWLink – NetWare Link

O

OEM – Original Equipment Manufacturer
OU – Organizational Unit

P

PCI – Peripheral Component Interconnect
PDC – Primary Domain Controller
PING – Packet Internetwork Groper
PPP – Point-to-Point Protocol
PPTP – Point-to-Point Tunneling Protocol
PWS – Peer Web Services

R

RADIUS – Remote Authentication Dial-in User Service
RAID-5 – RAID level 5
RAS – Remote Access Service
RC – Recovery Console
RFC – Request for Comment
RIS – Remote Installation Service
RRAS – Routing and Remote Access Service

S

SAM – Security Account Manager
SCSI – Small Computer System Interface
SCTS – Security Configuration Tool Set
SID – Security ID
SMS – Systems Management Server
SMTP – Simple Mail Transfer Protocol
SMW – Setup Manager Wizard
SNMP – Simple Network Management Protocol
SOHO – Small Office, Home Office
SPE – System Policy Editor
SSL – Secure Sockets Layer

T

TCP – Transport Control Protocol
TCO – Total Cost of Ownership

U

UDDW – Update Device Driver Wizard
URL – Uniform Resource Locator

USB – Universal Serial Bus

V

VPN – Virtual Private Network

W

WAN – Wide Area Network
WINS – Windows Internet Naming Service
WU – Windows Update
WWW – World Wide Web

ANSWER KEY

Section 1.0

Objective 1.1

Practice Questions:

1. c
2. a, d
3. b
4. b, c, d
5. b
6. a

Objective 1.2

Practice Questions:

1. b
2. d
3. a, c
4. a
5. b, d

Objective 1.3

Practice Questions:

1. a, c, d
2. b
3. b
4. a, b, c
5. c

Objective 1.4

Practice Questions:

1. a, b
2. c
3. a
4. a, b, c
5. a
6. b

Objective 1.5

Practice Questions:

1. c
2. a, b
3. c
4. c
5. b

Objective 1.6

Practice Questions:

1. a, c
2. c
3. a, b, c
4. c
5. a, b, c, d

Objective 1.7

Practice Questions:

1. a
2. d
3. a, b, c
4. b
5. a
6. b

Section 2.0

Objective 2.1

Practice Questions:

1. d
2. c
3. a, b, d
4. c
5. b
6. a, b, c
7. c

Objective 2.2

Practice Questions:

1. d
2. c, d
3. d
4. c, d
5. c
6. c
7. d

Objective 2.3

Practice Questions:

1. a
2. a, d
3. c
4. b
5. a
6. b
7. c

Objective 2.4

Practice Questions:

1. d
2. c
3. b

Objective 2.5

Practice Questions:

1. a
2. d
3. a, d
4. a
5. a
6. b, d
7. c

Objective 2.6

Practice Questions:

1. b
2. d
3. c
4. b
5. c
6. c

Objective 2.7

Practice Questions:

1. d
2. c
3. c
4. c
5. a, c
6. c, d

Objective 2.8

Practice Questions:

1. d
2. d
3. c
4. b
5. b

Objective 2.9

Practice Questions:

1. a, b, c, d
2. b
3. c
4. d
5. d
6. a
7. d

Objective 2.10

Practice Questions:

1. a
2. d, e
3. b
4. c
5. e

Objective 2.11

Practice Questions:

1. c
2. b
3. c
4. a
5. b
6. b
7. d

Objective 2.12

Practice Questions:

1. b
2. a
3. c
4. b
5. a
6. c
7. a

Objective 2.13

Practice Questions:

1. b
2. b
3. a, c, d
4. c
5. b, c
6. b

Objective 2.14

Practice Questions:

1. b
2. a
3. a, c
4. a, b
5. a, b
6. a
7. c
8. a

Objective 2.15

Practice Questions:

1. b
2. b
3. a
4. a
5. a, c
6. b
7. a

Objective 2.16

Practice Questions:

1. a, d, e
2. c
3. a, d
4. b
5. a
6. b, c

Objective 2.17

Practice Questions:

1. a
2. b
3. c, d
4. a
5. a, b, c, d

Objective 2.18

Practice Questions:

1. b
2. d
3. a
4. a, c
5. b
6. c

Objective 2.19

Practice Questions:

1. a
2. d
3. c
4. a, d
5. a, c
6. b, c

Objective 2.20

Practice Questions:

1. a
2. c
3. a, d
4. a, d
5. a, b, d
6. d

Objective 2.21

Practice Questions:

1. d
2. a
3. d
4. a
5. a
6. a, b, c
7. a

Objective 2.22

Practice Questions:

1. b
2. d
3. a
4. a, b, c
5. a
6. c, d
7. a, b, d, c

Objective 2.23

Practice Questions:

1. a
2. c
3. a
4. b
5. b, c, d
6. d
7. a

Objective 2.24

Practice Questions:

1. b
2. c
3. d
4. b
5. d
6. b

Objective 2.25

Practice Questions:

1. a
2. d
3. d
4. d
5. c

Objective 2.26

Practice Questions:

1. c
2. a, c
3. b, c
4. d

Objective 2.27

Practice Questions:

1. b
2. b
3. c
4. b
5. a

Section 3.0

Objective 3.1

Practice Questions:

1. a, b, c
2. a
3. a, b, c, d
4. Server 1(d); Server 2(a); Server 3(a); Server 4(c); Server 5(b)
5. c

Objective 3.2

Practice Questions:

1. c
2. a
3. c
4. a, b, c

Objective 3.3

Practice Questions:

1. b
2. c
3. b
4. b, c

Objective 3.4

Practice Questions:

1. a, b
2. a, b
3. a
4. b

Section 4.0

Objective 4.1

Practice Questions:

1. a, d
2. a, c
3. b
4. d
5. b
6. a

Objective 4.2

Practice Questions:

1. a
2. a, b, c, d
3. a
4. c, d
5. c

Objective 4.3

Practice Questions:

1. c
2. d
3. a
4. a
5. d

Objective 4.4

Practice Questions:

1. a
2. b
3. a, c
4. d
5. b
6. b
7. a

Objective 4.5

Practice Questions:

1. a
2. c
3. d
4. a
5. a
6. a
7. a, c, d

Objective 4.6

Practice Questions:

1. c, d
2. b
3. b, d
4. a, c, d
5. a, b, c

Objective 4.7

Practice Questions:

1. b, c, d
2. b, c
3. a
4. a, b, c, d
5. b
6. c
7. a, c

Objective 4.8

Practice Questions:

1. d
2. c
3. b
4. c
5. a, b, d
6. a
7. d

Objective 4.9

Practice Questions:

1. a, c, d
2. c
3. 1-a, b; 2-a, d; 3-a, b, d, e; 4-d, e; 5-c; 6-e
4. b
5. c

Objective 4.10

Practice Questions:

1. b, c
2. b
3. a
4. c, d, g
5. c

Objective 4.11

Practice Questions:

1. c, d, e, f
2. a, d
3. b
4. a, d, e, g
5. b
6. a, c

Section 5.0

Objective 5.1

Practice Questions:

1. a
2. c
3. a
4. b

Objective 5.2

Practice Questions:

1. a
2. b
3. c
4. c

Objective 5.3

Practice Questions:

1. c
2. d
3. c
4. d
5. b
6. a

Objective 5.4

Practice Questions:

1. a
2. c
3. b
4. d
5. b
6. a

Objective 5.5

Practice Questions:

1. d
2. c
3. a, b
4. b

Objective 5.6

Practice Questions:

1. d
2. b
3. a, c
4. b
5. d

Objective 5.7

Practice Questions:

1. a
2. b
3. b
4. a

Section 6.0

Objective 6.1

Practice Questions:

1. a, b, d, e, f
2. a, g
3. a, b, d

Objective 6.2

Practice Questions:

1. b
2. a
3. b, c
4. d
5. c

Objective 6.3

Practice Questions:

1. a
2. b
3. b
4. b
5. d
6. d
7. b

Objective 6.4

Practice Questions:

1. a
2. c
3. b

Objective 6.5

Practice Questions:

1. d
2. a
3. c
4. b
5. c
6. c

Objective 6.6

Practice Questions:

1. b, d
2. a
3. a, b
4. b, c, d

Objective 6.7

Practice Questions:

1. a
2. c, e

Objective 6.8

Practice Questions:

1. c
2. a
3. b
4. a, b, d, e
5. b, c, d
6. b
7. c

Objective 6.9

Practice Questions:

1. b
2. a, b
3. a
4. a, c, d
5 a
6. b
7. b

Objective 6.10

Practice Questions:

1. c
2. c
3. b
4. b
5. d

Objective 6.11

Practice Questions:

1. c
2. d
3. a
4. b, c
5. c
6. c, d

Objective 6.12

Practice Questions:

1. c
2. a
3. a
4. b
5. a, b, c, d

Objective 6.13

Practice Questions:

1. b, d, f, g, i, k
2. a, c, d, f
3. a
4. a, b, c, d

Objective 6.14

Practice Questions:

1. d
2. a
3. b
4. a, b, d, f

Objective 6.15

Practice Questions:

1. c
2. a
3. b
4. a, c, d
5. b
6. c
7. d

Objective 6.16

Practice Questions:

1. c
2. d
3. b
4. b, c, e, g
5. c

Objective 6.17

Practice Questions:

1. b, d, e
2. c
3. b
4. b
5. c
6. a
7. a, b

Objective 6.18

Practice Questions:

1. b, d
2. a, b
3. b
4. a, b, c, e, g
5. a, d
6. a

Section 7.0

Objective 7.1

Practice Questions:

1. b
2. d
3. b
4. b, c
5. b

Objective 7.2

Practice Questions:

1. c
2. d
3. c
4. a
5. a, b, c, d, e
6. a

Objective 7.3

Practice Questions:

1. a
2. b
3. c
4. a

Objective 7.4

Practice Questions:

1. c
2. b
3. a, b
4. d

Objective 7.5

Practice Questions:

1. a, b
2. c
3. b
4. c
5. a

Objective 7.6

Practice Questions:

1. d
2. b, c
3. a
4. b

Objective 7.7

Practice Questions:

1. b
2. b
3. a, b, d
4. b
5. d
6. a, b, c, d

Objective 7.8

Practice Questions:

1. b
2. b
3. c
4. c
5. d
6. a

Objective 7.9

Practice Questions:

1. b
2. b, c, d
3. a, b, d
4. c, d
5. d

Objective 7.10

Practice Questions:

1. a, b, c, d, e, f, g
2. a
3. b
4. d
5. a